→INTRODUCING

# FEMINISM

**CATHIA JENAINATI & JUDY GROVES**

Published in the UK in 2010
by Icon Books Ltd.,
Omnibus Business Centre,
39-41 North Road, London N7 9DP
email: info@iconbooks.co.uk
www.introducingbooks.com

Sold in the UK, Europe, South Africa
and Asia by Faber and Faber Ltd.,
Bloomsbury House,
74-77 Great Russell Street,
London WC1B 3DA
or their agents

Distributed in the UK, Europe,
South Africa and Asia by TBS Ltd.,
TBS Distribution Centre,
Colchester Road, Frating Green,
Colchester CO7 7DW

This edition published in Australia
in 2010 by Allen & Unwin Pty. Ltd.,
PO Box 8500, 83 Alexander Street,
Crows Nest, NSW 2065

Previously published in 2007

This edition published in the USA
in 2010 by Totem Books
Inquiries to: Icon Books Ltd.,
Omnibus Business Centre,
39-41 North Road,
London N7 9DP, UK

Distributed to the trade in the USA
by National Book Network Inc.,
4501 Forbes Boulevard, Suite 200,
Lanham, Maryland 20706

Distributed in Canada by
Penguin Books Canada,
90 Eglinton Avenue East, Suite 700,
Toronto, Ontario M4P 2Y3

ISBN: 978-184831-121-3

Originating editor: Richard Appignanesi

Printed by Gutenberg Press, Malta

# What is Feminism?

Any attempt to "introduce feminism" invariably faces numerous challenges. Where to start, who to include, what to leave out and when to stop are all important considerations. This book provides an overview of the development of feminist activism in the Anglo-speaking world. It specifically outlines feminist thought in Britain and the US, although it refers to international contexts where relevant.

The book acknowledges and intends to celebrate the variety of feminist perspectives which have developed throughout women's history, taking as its premise bell hooks' famous definition.

> FEMINISM IS THE STRUGGLE TO END SEXIST OPPRESSION.

BELL HOOKS

*Introducing Feminism* traces the historical and social development of this struggle.

# What is Patriarchy?

One starting point for thinking about feminist activity is coming to a consensus about what the term "patriarchy" means. A useful definition is provided by Chris Weedon.

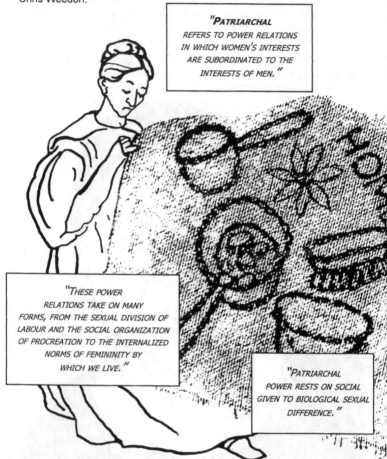

"*PATRIARCHAL* REFERS TO POWER RELATIONS IN WHICH WOMEN'S INTERESTS ARE SUBORDINATED TO THE INTERESTS OF MEN."

"*THESE POWER* RELATIONS TAKE ON MANY FORMS, FROM THE SEXUAL DIVISION OF LABOUR AND THE SOCIAL ORGANIZATION OF PROCREATION TO THE INTERNALIZED NORMS OF FEMININITY BY WHICH WE LIVE."

"*PATRIARCHAL* POWER RESTS ON SOCIAL GIVEN TO BIOLOGICAL SEXUAL DIFFERENCE."

The term "feminism" came into English usage around the 1890s, but women's conscious struggle to resist discrimination and sexist oppression goes much further back.

# Biology is Destiny

As early as the 4th century BC, **Aristotle** (384–322 BC) declared that "women were women by virtue of a certain lack of qualities". His predecessor the Greek historian and army general **Thucydides** (c. 460–400 BC) had some advice for women.

THUCYDIDES

> IT IS A GREAT GLORY IN A WOMAN TO SHOW NO MORE WEAKNESS THAN IS NATURAL TO HER SEX, AND NOT BE TALKED OF, EITHER FOR GOOD OR EVIL BY MEN.

Early thinking about the difference between women and men was based on **essentialist** ideas about gender which maintained that women's and men's differences are a result of biology. The belief that biology is destiny suggests that, in comparable situations, men exhibit "masculine" psychological traits such as aggressiveness, rationality and assertiveness, whereas women will exhibit "feminine" traits such as gentleness, intuitiveness and sensitivity. These differences, it was believed, translated into particular patterns of thought, feeling and behaviour specific to each gender.

# Logic or Emotion?

Essentialism sees men as able to think logically, abstractly and analytically, while women are mainly emotional, compassionate and nurturing creatures.

Essentialist thinking had repercussions on women's private and public lives. In private, essentialist ideas were translated into rules of conduct for the woman as wife, mother and daughter. In public, it was believed that women's participation should be limited and strictly controlled by a masculine representative of authority such as husband, father, the clergy, the law.

Essentialist ideas about women permeated Western thought for centuries and proposed that there is a natural, biologically determined essence of the feminine that is universal and unchangeable.

*"WOMAN IS FICKLE AND ALWAYS CHANGING."*

**VIRGIL** *(70–19 BC)*

*"WOMAN IS AN IMPERFECT MAN."*

**THOMAS AQUINAS**

*(1225–74)*

And **William Shakespeare's** (1564–1616) Hamlet famously exclaimed:

*"FRAILTY, THY NAME IS WOMAN!"*

Feminists have long fought to dispel such myths about gender.

# Early Modern Feminist Activity

Early Modern (1550–1700) English society was founded on the rule of the father.

Women had no formal rights and were not represented in the law. Even if some women were able to receive a higher education, they were not allowed to receive the degree for which they studied. In marriage, the woman's body belonged to her husband, who was also the only legal guardian of the children.

Early Modern feminist activity aimed at challenging the prevalent social view that women are weak and irrational creatures who should be controlled by men. There were a number of political events which supported such efforts, in particular Queen Elizabeth I's accession to the throne in 1558 and her long and successful reign as a single female.

# Reinterpreting the Bible

Writing on women's issues in the late 16th century began to proliferate, with a number of essays challenging the ideal of the female as "chaste, silent and obedient". In 1589, **Jane Anger**'s *Her Protection for Women* reinterpreted Genesis.

> IF GOD CREATED MAN FROM DUST, THEN HE MADE WOMAN FROM THE MAN'S BODY ...

> CONSEQUENTLY WOMEN ARE PURER AND MORE EXCELLENT BEINGS THAN MEN.

**Rachel Speght**'s *A Muzzle for Melastomus* (1617) questioned the story of Adam's fall from the Garden of Eden, taking issue with the underlying assumption that Adam had been seduced by Eve to eat the apple: "If Adam has not approved of that deed which Eve has done, and been willing to tread the steps which she had gone, he being her head would have reproved her."

The gender of authors such as Jane Anger, Rachel Speght, **Esther Sowernam** and **Sarah Egerton** remains debatable. Some critics believe them to be pseudonyms used to engage in literary debates rather than political reform. However, there was clearly concern with, and an active desire to challenge, traditional perceptions of women.

### Independent Churchwomen

Lawrence Stone, writing about the political and socio-economic status of women in 17th-century England, suggests that even as far back as the Civil War of the 1640s, women played an important role in religious interpretation by participating in independent churches where they were allowed to debate, to vote and even prophesy. These women sought to re-invent their roles by claiming a prominent position in society and religion.

> WE WILL NOT BE WIVES AND TIE UP OUR LIVES TO VILLAINOUS SLAVERY.

# First Political Action

In 1642, impoverished women working in a variety of trades collectively rebelled and marched into London to petition the Houses of Lords and Commons. They wanted the law to take into account their status of working individuals and to improve the conditions of the working class. Upon seeing them, the Duke of Richmond allegedly ordered (sarcastically) …

*AWAY WITH THESE WOMEN, WE WERE BEST HAVE A PARLIAMENT OF WOMEN.*

At this point, it is believed that the mob of nearly 400 women attacked him physically and broke his staff of office.

English working women continued to protest whenever political decisions discriminated against them or their class. Although these early efforts cannot be termed "feminist" in the contemporary sense of the word, yet these women's collective sentiment of injustice and their determination to fight unjust laws testifies to a **feminine consciousness** which united them.

## "To the Ladies"

In 1688, the "Glorious Revolution" saw the rejection of monarchical patriarchy with the overthrow of James II, initiating a fierce wave of publications by literary women such as **Aphra Behn** (1640–89) and **Lady Chudleigh** (1656–1710), whose 1703 poem "To the Ladies" expresses the feelings of the era:

To the Ladies
Wife and servant are the same,
But only differ in the name.

When the word "obey" has said,
And man by law supreme has made,

Fierce as an Eastern Prince he grows
And all his innate rigor shows.

Then shun, oh shun that wretched state
And all the fawning flatterers hate.
Value yourselves and men despise:
You must be proud if you'll be wise.

# Early Perspectives

### The Society of Friends

In 1652, the Society of Friends was founded in England by Quakers. Quakers do not accept any form of hierarchy between people. They do not take their hat off to anyone, as was demonstrated in the meeting of the prominent Quaker William Penn and the French King Charles II.

*I REFUSED TO REMOVE MY HAT AND EXPLAINED TO THE KING THAT QUAKERS UNCOVER THEMSELVES ONLY TO THE LORD.*

WILLIAM PENN

This belief in social equality was unique for its time, and was translated into a series of original attitudes towards race and gender. Between 1755 and 1776, Quakers became active in fighting the institution of slavery by creating abolition societies to promote emancipation.

Within the family, Quakers did not differentiate between the social roles of men and women. As a result, many female Friends were highly educated and played prominent roles in politics and education. Quaker women would travel unaccompanied, contribute to Church administration and preach to mixed audiences.

Consequently it is believed that in the 19th century "Quaker women comprised 40 per cent of female abolitionists, 19 per cent of feminists born before 1830, and 15 per cent of suffragists born before 1830". (Mary Maples)

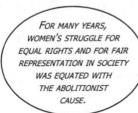

*FOR MANY YEARS, WOMEN'S STRUGGLE FOR EQUAL RIGHTS AND FOR FAIR REPRESENTATION IN SOCIETY WAS EQUATED WITH THE ABOLITIONIST CAUSE.*

# The Age of Reason

During the 18th and 19th centuries, many notable female figures were outspoken about the need to challenge women's subordinate social position. Their writings express, to a great extent, the legacy of the Age of Enlightenment by insisting that we must use **reason** as opposed to **faith** to discover any truth about our existence. Finding things out individually rather than unquestioningly following tradition was the Enlightenment's practice of **free enquiry**.

# Social Planners

One consequence of the Enlightenment's emphasis on the rational is the impulse towards **social planning**. The social planners believed it to be their duty to plan and order the world around them. The Anglo-American social reformer **Frances Wright** (1795–1852) attempted to model this belief when she set up her own experimental community, **Nashoba**, dedicated to ensuring the emancipation of slaves.

Wright believed that for women as for slaves, more schooling and less churchgoing would ensure independence and guarantee happiness. Several factors contributed to the failure of this ambitious experiment ...

*SWAMP FEVER ...*

*NEGATIVE PUBLICITY ...*

*AND ANTAGONISM FROM THE GENERAL PUBLIC.*

As a social planner, Wright stands apart from many of her contemporaries for being particularly concerned with the plight of the working class. She advocated abolition, universal education, birth control and equal rights for women.

The ideas of the Enlightenment translated into yet another perspective. Harriet Martineau and John Stuart Mill (see pages 60–1 and 40–6) are two thinkers who put great emphasis on the power of thought and education to release the individual from the ghost of **tradition**. But they spoke mainly to an elite social audience in spite of their attempts to put their theories into action.

## Competing Perspectives

In the Anglo-American tradition, early thinking about women followed broadly two strategies:

The **relational perspective** proposed a vision of an egalitarian society based on non-hierarchical gender difference with the male–female couple as its basic unit.

IT DEFINED WOMEN'S RIGHTS IN RELATION TO WOMEN'S UNIQUE CONTRIBUTION TO THE COMMONWEALTH AND THEIR CHILDBEARING AND NURTURING CAPACITIES.

The **individualist perspective** posited the individual as the basic unit of society.

IT EMPHASIZED THE INDIVIDUAL'S NEED FOR PERSONAL FULFILMENT AND AUTONOMY WHILE DOWNPLAYING ALL SOCIALLY CONSTRUCTED NOTIONS OF GENDER IDENTITY.

# The Rise of Individualism

Social activity and philosophical writing on women was founded on either of these ways of thinking, although many writers often used a combination of both. Between 1890 and 1920, both perspectives seemed complementary. But by 1920, their goals had diverged, reflecting women's varied needs and experiences.

Individualism's respect for human rights and its dismissive attitude towards sex-linked qualities was the representative way of thinking for the post-Second World War generation of women.

# First Wave Feminism

We think of **first wave feminism** as referring to the **organized** feminist activity which evolved in Britain and the USA in the second half of the 19th century. This organized movement relied primarily on the various independent and sporadic activities of 18th-century feminists.

They were not particularly concerned with working-class women, and did not label themselves as feminists (a term coined in 1895). They were mostly concerned with injustices that they had experienced on a personal basis.

The major achievements of the first wave feminists were: the opening of higher education to women and the reform of secondary education for girls; and the enactment of the Married Women's Property Act, 1870. They remained active until the outbreak of the First World War in 1914, which put a stop to suffrage campaigns. First wave feminist activism failed to secure the vote.

## Milestones of First Wave Feminism

**1770-84** Abigail Adams corresponds with her husband
**1792** Mary Wollstonecraft, *A Vindication of the Rights of Woman*
**1821** Frances Wright, *Views of Society and Manners in America*
**1837** Harriet Martineau, *Society in America*
**1837** Angelina Grimké lectures in public about abolition and women's suffrage
**1837** Lucretia Mott and Elizabeth Cady attend World Anti-Slavery Convention in London
**1848** Seneca Falls Convention
**1851** Harriet Taylor Mill, "The Enfranchisement of Women"
**1854** Caroline Norton, *English Laws for Women in the 19th Century*
**1866** Barbara Bodichon founds Women's Suffrage Committee
**1869** John Stuart Mill, "The Subjection of Women"
**1869** Married Women's Property Act
**1892** New Zealand grants women's suffrage
**1902** Women's Suffrage Conference held in Washington DC
**1903** Emmeline Pankhurst founds the Woman's Social and Political Union (WSPU)
**1905** Vida Goldstein founds *Women's Sphere*
**1909** Vida Goldstein founds *Woman Voter*
**1914-18** First World War

FRIEDRICH ENGELS

IN 1884 FRIEDRICH ENGELS WROTE *THE ORIGINS OF THE FAMILY, PRIVATE PROPERTY AND THE STATE*. IN THIS WORK HE ARGUES THAT THE FAMILY UNIT IS VITAL FOR THE SUCCESS OF CAPITALISM.

# Remembering the Ladies

Back in the late 18th century, individualist and relational perspectives of thinking about women were already combined in Abigail Adams's view of gender relations.

**Abigail Adams** (1744–1818), wife of John Adams, the second President of the USA, was one of the most influential women of her day. During the American Revolution (1775–83), she and her husband lived apart by virtue of his political commitments. She wrote to him regularly and urged him to "remember to think about the Ladies" while drafting the Declaration of Independence. Her letters were compiled and published posthumously by her grandson.

In addition to demanding equal representation for women within the law, Adams also warned against depriving women of access to education and social equality. "If you complain of neglect of education in sons, what shall I say with regard to daughters? I most sincerely wish … that our new Constitution may be distinguished for encouraging learning and virtue."

Her opinions, though influential in small circles, remained largely unheard. Two months before the Declaration of Independence was written, she complained that "whilst you are proclaiming peace and good will to men, emancipating all nations, you insist upon retaining absolute power over your wives. But you must remember that arbitrary power is most like other things which are very hard, very liable to be broken."

# Mary Wollstonecraft

Abigail Adams was not the only female voice warning against the dangers of perpetuating social and legal discrimination against women. In 1792, the English writer **Mary Wollstonecraft** (1759–97), who was influenced by the ideas of the American and French Revolutions, called for the full participation of women in the rights and duties of citizenship.

*LIKE OTHER EARLY ENGLISH FEMINISTS, I EQUATE MASCULINE POWER WITH POLITICAL TYRANNY.*

MARY WOLLSTONECRAFT

The publication of Wollstonecraft's *A Vindication of the Rights of Woman* (1792) is generally thought to be the first conscious attempt at engaging polemically with issues of gender discrimination.

# An Unconventional Life

Wollstonecraft led an unconventional life by the standards of her time. She was born into an impoverished family and had to take up several jobs as a lady's companion and then governess to support herself. She began writing aged nineteen, and published *Thoughts on the Education of Daughters* (1787) in which she described the situation of educated young girls like herself who were forced to work for "rich fools".

Wollstonecraft fell deeply in love with the married painter and philosopher **Henri Fuseli**. She did not reveal her passion to him, preferring instead to escape to France where she met and became enamoured of the American author **Gilbert Imlay**.

WILLIAM GODWIN

*I DECLARED MYSELF IMLAY'S WIFE AND HAD A CHILD WITH HIM OUT OF WEDLOCK.*

When the relationship with Imlay broke down, she was consoled by the political writer and long-time friend **William Godwin**, with whom she began a passionate relationship which soon resulted in another pregnancy. Wollstonecraft convinced Godwin to get married in order to save her reputation. She died ten days after giving birth to her second daughter, **Mary Godwin** (later Mary Shelley, author of *Frankenstein*).

# Against Rousseau

Wollstonecraft wrote *Vindication* in response to the Swiss-French philosopher **Jean-Jacques Rousseau** (1712–78), whose book *Emile* claimed that women were sentimental and frivolous, and that in marriage they could occupy only a subordinate position as companions to their husbands.

As a pioneer of the British suffrage movement she was outspoken about the need to challenge prescribed gender roles. She advocated women's education and argued for their right to participate in public life, declaring:

*I DO NOT WISH WOMEN TO TAKE POWER OVER MEN; BUT OVER THEMSELVES.*

# Sense and Sensibility

As a **liberal feminist**, Wollstonecraft believed that it was the state's responsibility to protect civil liberties such as the right to vote, the right to own property and freedom of speech.

*AS LONG AS WOMEN ARE PROHIBITED FROM MAKING THEIR OWN DECISIONS, THEY WILL LACK LIBERTY ...*

*AND BECAUSE THEY ARE DISCOURAGED FROM DEVELOPING THEIR POWERS OF REASON, THEY WILL LACK VIRTUE.*

Hence, when society denies women the chance to develop their rational powers, to become moral persons who are involved in social commitments, it also denies them basic civil liberties.

In this respect, teaching girls to read romance, play music, sing and recite poetry will nourish their sensibilities at the cost of their sense. Girls educated in such frivolous pursuits, she concluded, are more likely to become emotionally dependent, to shirk their domestic duties and indulge in morally reprehensible actions. Rational and independent women however, develop moral capacities which enable them to become "observant daughters", "affectionate sisters", "reasonable mothers" and "faithful wives".

# The Divine Right of Husbands

Wollstonecraft maintained that an ideal marriage is one of intellectual companionship and equality. She challenged contemporary social beliefs by declaring that:

*THE DIVINE RIGHT OF HUSBANDS, LIKE THE DIVINE RIGHTS OF KINGS, MAY, IT IS HOPED, IN THIS ENLIGHTENED AGE, BE CONTESTED WITHOUT DANGER.*

The strength of Wollstonecraft's analysis is that it argues for the necessity of educating women to enable them to achieve economic independence. However, her arguments which privilege traits traditionally associated with males, and invite women to adopt them, are limited in scope and nowadays seen as controversial. Wollstonecraft does not resolve the problem of women's lack of access to the public domain and her aspirations for women remain theoretical.

In England, the effects of Wollstonecraft's *Vindication* were undermined by the subsequent publication of her *Memoirs* (1798), which were authored by her husband. As a single mother who refused to marry until late in life and who twice attempted to commit suicide, Wollstonecraft's life was all but conventional, as we have seen. The *Memoirs* exaggerated details of her personal life which were deemed immoral and controversial.

In addition, her passionate claims to sexual equality and her sympathy for the French Revolution alienated her supporters. **Horace Walpole** famously referred to her as ...

*THAT HYENA IN PETTICOATS.*

As a result, *Vindication* went out of print until 1844 and Wollstonecraft herself was regarded as a dire warning against uncontrolled emotionalism.

# The Grimké Sisters

Abigail Adams and Mary Wollstonecraft were not isolated voices.
**Angelina Grimké** (1805–79), a lecturer for the American Anti-Slavery Society and a public speaker on women's rights, found herself the focus of attention as one of the first women to speak out in the USA. She urged women, who could not vote or take part in political decisions, to make their voices heard by writing petitions to Congress. In a public lecture in 1838, she warned her female audience that:

ANGELINA GRIMKÉ

*MEN WHO HOLD THE ROD OVER SLAVES, RULE IN THE COUNCILS OF THE NATION: AND THEY DENY OUR RIGHT TO PETITION AND TO REMONSTRATE AGAINST ABUSES OF OUR SEX AND OUR KIND.*

She urged them to look to England, where "women did much to abolish Slavery in her colonies" by petitioning Queen Victoria. Grimké insisted that if women united in petitioning for their rights, it would be impossible for Congress to ignore them.

In 1838, she became the first woman in the US to be allowed to address a law-making body.

Her sister **Sarah Grimké** (1792–1873) was also a spokesperson for the abolitionist cause and for women's rights. The sisters' repeated public appearances defied accepted standards of the time and caused outrage in social circles. Their affirmation that men and women are created equal and that women should be allowed the same social and civil liberties as men created a general public uproar. They were criticised by clergy members for behaving like men.

In one of the letters she wrote to Catherine Beecher, Angelina Grimké echoed Abigail Adams's warning about a women's uprising:

# The "Cult of Domesticity", 1820–80

Social reformists in England and the US attempted to make their voices heard by staging numerous public lectures, founding societies and writing extensively about the "woman question". Most notably, the Anglo-American author Frances Wright, founder of the Nashoba commune, toured the US from 1818 to 1820 and reported her impressions in *Views of Society and Manners in America* (1821). She became an active member of American literary circles and published extensively on the importance of universal education, birth control and equal rights for women.

FRANCES WRIGHT

The obstacles that early activists were trying to overcome were significant. The years 1820–80 were still largely dominated by publications which depicted stereotypical representations of women. Advice manuals, literature books and public sermons contributed to the perpetuation of a **cult of domesticity** which ascribed to women a strictly private function and to men a public role. Any suggestion of crossing gender boundaries was considered a threat to the stability of the social hierarchy. One example offers a case in point.

In England, the publication of Godwin's scandalous *Memoirs* of Mary Wollstonecraft in 1798 was followed by a wave of books reacting against Wollstonecraft's ideas – most notably, **Sarah Ellis**'s *Women of England*, *The Mothers of England* and *The Daughters of England*.

# Rules of Conduct for Men and Women

**Matthew Carey** was an Irish-born publisher who lived in Philadelphia and wrote about various moral and education issues. In 1830 he published an essay entitled "Rules for Husbands and Wives" in which he advised husbands to treat their wives as equals. He summarized his recommendations into maxims and emphasized that "Bear and Forebear" is the best counsel for a happy marriage.

*1. A good husband will always regard his wife as his equal; treat her with kindness, respect and attention; and never address her with an air of authority, as if she were, as some husbands appear to regard their wives, a mere housekeeper.*

*2. He will never interfere in her domestic concerns, hiring servants, &c.*

*3. He will always keep her liberally supplied with money for furnishing his table in a style proportioned to his means, and for the purchase of dress suitable to her station in life.*

*4. He will cheerfully and promptly comply with all her reasonable requests, when it can be done, without loss, or great inconvenience.*

*5. He will never allow himself to lose his temper towards her, by indifferent cookery, or irregularity in the hours of meals, or any other mismanagement of her servants, knowing the difficulty of making them do their duty.*

*6. If she have prudence and good sense, he will consult her on all great operations, involving the risque of ruin, or serious injury in case of failure. Many a man has been rescued from destruction by the wise counsels of his wife. Many a foolish husband has most seriously injured himself and family by the rejection of the advice of his wife, fearing, lest, if he followed it, he would be regarded as ruled by her! A husband can never procure a counsellor more deeply interested in his welfare than his wife.*

*7. If distressed, or embarrassed in his circumstances, he will communicate his situation to her with candour, that she may bear his difficulties in mind, in her expenditures. Women sometimes, believing their husband's circumstances to be far better than they really are, expend money which cannot well be afforded, and which, if they knew their real situation, they would shrink from expending.*

1. *A good wife will always receive her husband with smiles – leave nothing undone to render home agreeable – and gratefully reciprocate his kindness and attention.*

2. *She will study to discover the means to gratify his inclinations, in regard to food and cookery; in the management of her family; in her dress, manners and deportment.*

3. *She will never attempt to rule, or appear to rule her husband. Such conduct degrades husbands — and wives always partake largely of the degradation of their husbands.*

4. *She will, in every thing reasonable, comply with his wishes – and, as far as possible, anticipate them.*

5. *She will avoid all altercations or arguments leading to ill-humour – and more especially before company.*

6. *She will never attempt to interfere in his business, unless he ask her advice or counsel, and will never attempt to control him in the management of it.*

*Should differences arise between husband and wife, the contest ought to be, not who will display the most spirit, but who will make the first advances. There is scarcely a more prolific source of unhappiness in the married state, than this "spirit", the legitimate offspring of pride and want of feeling.*

Carey's advice attempted to emphasize the different spheres in which males and females dwell. Women should be restricted to household management tasks while men belong to the public sphere where they earn money in order to provide for their family. In spite of his emphasis on equality and respect between husbands and wives, Carey cannot help himself but establish a clear hierarchy in the relationship.

# Harriet Taylor Mill

**Harriet Taylor Mill** (1807–58) and **John Stuart Mill** (1806–73) are two key figures who endorsed Wollstonecraft's liberal feminist ideas and expanded on them in the second half of the 19th century. They too led an unconventional private life.

Harriet Taylor was married and mother to two children when she met J.S. Mill and began a long-term relationship with him – with the permission of her husband John Taylor. Harriet and Mill were attracted to each other intellectually and emotionally, although it is believed that their relationship remained Platonic until they were married following the death of John Taylor.

*I REMAINED DUTY-BOUND TO MY HUSBAND THROUGHOUT HIS LIFETIME, MAINTAINING A FAÇADE OF MARITAL BLISS AND PATIENTLY CARING FOR HIM DURING HIS ILLNESS.*

Early on in the courtship, J.S. Mill would visit Harriet and John Taylor's house nightly. Although Taylor was devoted to his wife, he would usually leave for his club to allow Harriet and Mill time alone.

However, when Taylor learned that he was terminally ill with cancer, he asked his wife to return home to care for him. Harriet found herself in a difficult situation because J.S. Mill was then suffering from an injured hip and temporary blindness, and needed her care. She did, however, devote herself to her husband and cared for him until his death.

## Theory and Practice

There is still uncertainty as to whether the Mills enjoyed a sexual relationship before or after their marriage. There is evidence in their writing to suggest that they found the sexual act inherently degrading. Other evidence suggests that J.S. Mill might have been impotent and that Harriet might have contracted syphilis from her first husband. Their anti-conventional lifestyle and questionable sexual relationship informs many of the essays on sexual equality which they published.

Two essays, one on "The Enfranchisement of Women" (1851), the other "On the Subjection of Women" (1869), illustrate their commitment to write about sexual discrimination from an informed perspective. The fact that they agree on principles and disagree on the solutions further testifies to their personal engagement with these issues.

Taylor is thought to be the primary author of the essay on the enfranchisement of women.

Taylor elaborated Wollstonecraft's call for women's education, adding that women must also be allowed to contribute to the labour market and to the legal and justice systems on an equal basis with men. She suggested that it was possible for women to reconcile motherhood with the demands of a professional life, and emphasized that work was necessary to maintain the sanity of woman.

# A Panoply of Servants

Similarly to Wollstonecraft, Taylor lucidly highlighted the social obstacles that isolated women and hindered any attempt at gaining equal status with men. However, and in a similar vein to her predecessor, Taylor's argument is very much a product of a particular social class.

LIKE WOLLSTONECRAFT, I ACKNOWLEDGE THAT THE DOMESTIC CHORES WHICH WOMEN ARE EXPECTED TO FULFIL ON A DAILY BASIS OCCUPY MOST OF THEIR TIME AND ENERGY.

BOTH OF US RECOGNIZE THE NEED FOR A PANOPLY OF DOMESTIC SERVANTS TO ASSIST IN THE RUNNING OF THE HOUSEHOLD.

Gaining an education and the ability to combine a career with marriage and motherhood were luxuries open only to the wealthy few who could afford them.

## "Man" or "Person"?

J.S. Mill's essay on the subjection of women established a correlation between the degree of civilization of a people and the social position of its women. He argued against essentialism.

*WHAT IS NOW CALLED THE NATURE OF WOMEN IS AN EMINENTLY ARTIFICIAL THING.*

*IT IS RIDICULOUS THAT ANY PERSON OR DOCTRINE CAN PURPORT TO "KNOW" THE NATURE OF THE TWO SEXES.*

Most importantly, Mill observed that unless women's efforts at engaging with intellectual debates and gaining an education are supported by society, their ideas will consist of a small component of individual observation and a large element of absorbed ideas, or imitations.

Upon becoming an MP, J.S. Mill introduced an amendment to the 1867 Reform Act by substituting the word "person" for the word "man". Although the amendment was defeated, it sparked a legal case to establish that words of the masculine gender should include women.

In spite of his challenging ideas, Mill curiously remarked that if women were given the opportunity to pursue a career, the majority would opt for a life of domesticity.

Taylor and Mill were social reformists. Their ideas were original and highly controversial for their time, but they still upheld many of the erroneous notions about gender which later critics will aim to dispel. For example, they both considered mothering as a superior and more natural practice to fathering; and they both challenged the division of labour within the family which ascribed particular roles to mothers and fathers, but neither offered a practical solution to it.

# Caroline Norton

While social reformists and political activists were busy writing, lecturing and debating the "woman question", individual cases where the law was being challenged were gradually being made public.

WE STARTED TO CAMPAIGN FOR PARTICULAR REFORMS, NOT BECAUSE WE SAW OURSELVES AS FEMINISTS, BUT BECAUSE PARTICULAR CIRCUMSTANCES IN OUR LIVES FORCED US TO PROTEST AND MAKE OUR VOICES HEARD.

the ... time hath wrought on love
he sno ... s summer prime),
hould a chance si ... or sudden tear-drop move
hy heart to memory ... f the olden time;
urn not to gaze on ... itying eyes,
Nor mock me w ... e renewed;
But from the ... ved, arise
And leave m ...
What boots ...
Shoots from ... ce it came,
We gaze upon ... nust expire:
And know the ... will break;
Therefore no pity, ...
Be cold, be careless — for thy past love's sake!

CAROLINE NORTON

**Lady Caroline Norton** (1808–77) was a novelist and poet who became a spokesperson for women's rights after her husband divorced her. Her battles for custody and property in 1839 were crucial controversies which highlighted the plight of mothers trapped in unhappy marriages.

# Coverture

In the early 19th century, married women in Europe and the USA had no legal identity apart from their husbands. This legal status was known as **coverture**. As a result of coverture, no woman was able to be party in a lawsuit, sit on a jury, own property if widowed, or write a will. In cases where custody of children was to be decided by the courts, this was usually granted to the children's father.

Caroline, who was renowned for her beauty and intellect, was married to George Norton, a slow-witted, violent and unfaithful man.

Although George Norton had initially encouraged this friendship, hoping to achieve high status for himself, he soon decided to end the marriage by suing Caroline for divorce and Lord Melbourne for "criminal conversation" – adultery.

# The Infant Custody Act

Consequently Caroline was refused access to their three children. George went on to ruin his wife's reputation by making allegations of her sexual emancipation and claiming that her success and strength of character were symptoms of her sexual transgressions. Caroline sought the help of a sergeant-at-law, who fought for an Infant Custody Bill in parliament while she wrote *A Plain Letter to the Lord Chancellor on the Infant Custody Bill* (1839).

*I ARGUED AGAINST AN UNJUST LAW WHICH DEPRIVED A MOTHER OF HER LEGITIMATE CHILDREN.*

This high-profile legal case resulted in the passing of the Infant Custody Act in 1839, allowing mothers of "irreproachable character" custody of children under the age of seven and regular access to older children.

# The Matrimonial Causes Act

While living on her own, Caroline Norton supported herself by writing. Yet, as *femme covert*, her earnings legally belonged to her husband.

IT WAS NOT UNTIL I WENT BACK TO COURT TO SUE HIM FOR NOT PAYING MY ANNUAL INCOME THAT MARRIED WOMEN'S PROPERTY REFORM WAS INITIATED.

Norton went on to conduct more research into women's legal status and eventually published *English Laws for Women in the Nineteenth Century* (1856). This, along with a petition signed by 25,000 women in favour of married women's property ownership, resulted in the Matrimonial Causes Act of 1857, the precursor of the 1870 act which allowed married women control over their financial earnings and inherited property.

What is fascinating about Norton's rhetoric is her insistence on the fact that she does not wish to transgress her position of female who remains in many ways subordinate to men in power. She cleverly constructs her essays as appeals to the protection of the law.

"Our mercantile and uncertain speculation of 'damages', – the wonderful indecency of our divorce trials, – the incredible fact that the woman accused is allowed no direct defence, and cannot appear by counsel on such occasions, – the loth and reluctant admission of the right of a mother to her infant children, – are alike odious and incomprehensible."

Caroline Norton's triumphs paved the way for more substantial reforms in the late 19th century. But the law remained mostly on the fathers' side, retaining the principles of inequality between women and men.

# Catherine Helen Spence

**Catherine Helen Spence** (1825–1910) was a Scottish-born Australian feminist who started her public career as a fiction writer. She also wrote literary criticism for the *South Australian Register* in 1872.

As a social reformer, Spence campaigned for girls' education, divorce law reform and women's suffrage.

*I BECAME AUSTRALIA'S FIRST FEMALE POLITICAL CANDIDATE WHEN I STOOD FOR THE FEDERAL CONVENTION HELD IN ADELAIDE IN 1897.*

CATHERINE HELEN SPENCE

She was not elected then, but gained a formidable reputation as a leading suffragette and social campaigner. She was known as the "Greatest Australian Woman" and the "Grand Old Woman of Australasia" and is commemorated on the five dollar banknote.

# Seneca Falls Convention, New York 1848

Meanwhile, in the US the fight for abolishing slavery was gaining momentum, and activists for women's suffrage were still allying their cause to that of the abolitionists. American suffragettes were also looking to establish links with their "sisters" in Europe.

In 1840 **Lucretia Mott** (1793–1880) and **Elizabeth Cady Stanton** (1815–1902) travelled to London to attend the World Anti-Slavery Convention.

When they returned to New York, they decided to organize a convention to which they invited women suffragists and interested men. The aim was to discuss issues related to equality in education, marriage and property laws. 53

This was the text of the invitation:

Woman's Rights Convention. – A Convention to discuss the social, civil, and religious condition and rights of woman, will be held in the Wesleyan Chapel, at Seneca Falls, N. Y., on Wednesday and Thursday, the 19th and 20th of July, current; commencing at 10 o'clock am. During the first day the meeting will be exclusively for women, who are earnestly invited to attend. The public generally are invited to be present on the second day, when Lucretia Mott, of Philadelphia, and other ladies and gentlemen, will address the convention.

Stanton gave the keynote speech, which she entitled "Now we demand our right to vote". She provocatively warned men in power that "so long as your women are slaves you may throw your colleges and churches to the winds".

YOU CAN'T HAVE SCHOLARS AND SAINTS SO LONG AS YOUR MOTHERS ARE GROUND TO POWDER BETWEEN THE UPPER AND NETHER MILLSTONE OF TYRANNY AND LUST.

# A Declaration of Independence

At the close of the convention, a "Declaration of Sentiments and Resolutions" was read out. Its style imitated and parodied the US Declaration of Independence, beginning with "We hold these truths to be self-evident: that all men and women are created equal". Eleven Resolutions were passed, including:

"Resolved, That all laws which prevent woman from occupying such a station in society as her conscience shall dictate, or which place her in a position inferior to that of man, are contrary to the great precept of nature, and therefore of no force or authority."

"Resolved, That woman is man's equal – was intended to be so by the Creator, and the highest good of the race demands that she should be recognized as such."

"Resolved, That it is the duty of the women of this country to secure to themselves the sacred right to the elective franchise."

Many historians cite Seneca Falls as the beginning of the first wave of feminist activity in the US, the main aim of which was to achieve suffrage for women; for with the vote women would be able to challenge unjust laws and participate in the implementations of new laws which guaranteed their rights.

# The Advent of the Bloomers

One year after Seneca Falls, American suffragettes used various means to draw public attention to unjust laws and discriminatory social standards. One notable suffragette was **Elizabeth Smith Miller**, who paraded the streets of Seneca Falls wearing a pair of "Turkish trousers". This fashion statement caught the attention of Amelia Jenks Bloomer, publisher and editor of the first American women's rights newspaper, *Lily*.

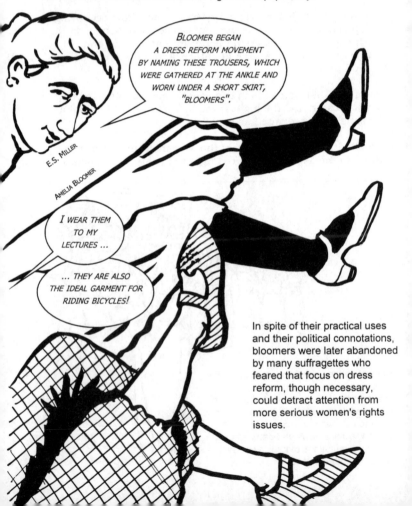

In spite of their practical uses and their political connotations, bloomers were later abandoned by many suffragettes who feared that focus on dress reform, though necessary, could detract attention from more serious women's rights issues.

# The 1850s in the USA

The 1850s were a period of great social and political change in the US. Two of the most notable female figures were Elizabeth Cady Stanton and **Susan B. Anthony** (1820–1906). Stanton campaigned for women's right over their reproduction, sexuality and divorce laws, and repeatedly reminded her audience of the slave-like status of women.

ELIZABETH CADY STANTON

THE NEGRO'S SKIN AND THE WOMEN'S SEX ARE PRIMA FACIE EVIDENCE THAT THEY WERE INTENDED TO BE SUBJECTED TO THE WHITE ANGLO-SAXON MAN.

Anthony was a liberal Quaker and a dedicated radical reformer. Her involvement in women's rights began in 1851 when she met Stanton. Together they organized the National Woman Suffrage Association and published a newspaper, *Revolution*, which made public various injustices suffered by women.

# The International Council of Women

To bring attention to their mission, Anthony defiantly registered and cast a ballot in the 1872 presidential elections.

In 1883 she went to Europe and met women's rights activists. She helped form the **International Council of Women** (1888) which included 49 delegates from nine countries: Canada, the US, Ireland, India, Britain, Finland, Denmark, France and Norway. The ICW's first meeting in Washington DC resulted in the drafting of a constitution. It held national and international meetings on a regular basis, and was a highly influential organization which encouraged the establishing of the first National Council of Women of Australia in New South Wales in 1896.

Anthony continued to speak at conventions until late in her life. In 1979, the US Mint honoured her work by issuing the Susan B. Anthony silver dollar coin.

ARE WOMEN PERSONS? AND I HARDLY BELIEVE ANY OF OUR OPPONENTS WILL HAVE THE HARDIHOOD TO SAY THEY ARE NOT.

BEING PERSONS, THEN, WOMEN ARE CITIZENS; AND NO STATE HAS A RIGHT TO MAKE ANY LAW, OR TO ENFORCE ANY OLD LAW, THAT SHALL ABRIDGE THEIR PRIVILEGES OR IMMUNITIES.

HENCE, EVERY DISCRIMINATION AGAINST WOMEN IN THE CONSTITUTIONS AND LAWS OF THE SEVERAL STATES IS TODAY NULL AND VOID ...

# The 1850s in Britain

The 1850s witnessed a resurgence of feminist activism in Britain, where a series of important legislations were introduced as a result of high-profile legal battles and in response to the growing number of single middle-class women who campaigned for economic independence. Among the key figures of this period were **Harriet Martineau** (1802–76) and **Barbara Leigh Smith Bodichon** (1827–91).

Harriet Martineau was born to Unitarian parents who held progressive views on girls' education.

HARRIET MARTINEAU

*I RECEIVED A SIMILAR EDUCATION TO MY BROTHERS, BUT WAS NOT ALLOWED TO ATTEND UNIVERSITY LIKE THEM.*

She protested against this in an anonymous publication entitled *On Female Education* (1823). This essay was praised by her brother James, who advised her: "Now, dear, leave it to the other women to make skirts and darn stockings, and you devote yourself to this."

Martineau devoted her life to writing about politics and economics, emphasizing the need for social reform. Upon returning from a trip to the USA (1834–6), she wrote about the *Political Non-existence of Women*, who, she observed, were being treated as slaves.

Throughout her life, she campaigned for equal employment opportunities and state education for girls. She also wrote in favour of allowing women to join the medical profession.

# Barbara Bodichon

Barbara Leigh Smith's background is fascinating. Her father, Benjamin Leigh Smith, came from a Unitarian radical family which had campaigned against the slave trade and supported the French Revolution. She was born as a result of her father's seducing seventeen-year-old Anne Longden, who remained Smith's common-law wife until her untimely death when Barbara was seven years old.

Barbara's father was an advocate of women's rights and encouraged his daughter's independence by providing her with £300 a year allowance.

*WITH THIS INCOME, I WAS ABLE TO MOVE TO LONDON AND PURSUE A SUCCESSFUL CAREER AS A WRITER AND ACTIVIST.*

Like Martineau, she wrote extensively in favour of women doctors and opportunities for women in higher education. She campaigned with Caroline Norton for changing legislation with regard to divorce and the protection of property rights of divorced women.

Although she had been against marriage by principle, Barbara decided to marry Eugene Bodichon, a former French army officer who held radical political views and supported her efforts for achieving women's rights.

In 1866 she formed the Women's Suffrage Committee. Its members penned a suffrage petition, signed by 1,500 women, which J.S. Mill agreed to present to the House of Commons on their behalf. On 7 June the committee chose **Emily Davies** and **Elizabeth Garrett** to carry the large roll of parchment into Westminster.

*IN ORDER TO AVOID DETECTION, I ASKED AN APPLE-WOMAN TO HIDE THE ROLL UNDER HER STAND.*

*UPON LEARNING OF ITS CONTENTS, I INSISTED ON ADDING MY SIGNATURE TO IT ...*

*... SO IT HAD TO BE UNFOLDED AGAIN.*

Bodichon is mostly remembered for her efforts in raising funds for the first women's college in Cambridge. Girton College was opened in 1873, although its female students were not allowed full participation in the university until 1948.

## Langham Place

The "Langham Place" circle was a group of middle-class activist women who discussed and published their views on women's rights. They met at 19 Langham Place in London, better known as the headquarters of first wave feminism. Two of their active members were Barbara Bodichon and **Bessie Rayner Parkes** (1829–1925), who established *The English Women's Review* and a Society for the Promoting of the Employment of Women.

64

Harriet Martineau wrote a memorable article entitled "Female Industry", arguing that a wider choice of professions should be made available to middle-class women.

THEY SHOULD BE TAUGHT THAT WORKING DOES NOT DEGRADE THEIR STATUS.

Martineau challenged the restrictive, socially-constructed understanding that a "lady" should not work and should remain "redundant", devoting herself to family and domesticity.

# Emmeline Pankhurst

The women's suffrage movement in Britain fought for a whole range of feminist demands, including: the right to vote, cooperative rather than family-based childcare, equal pay for women, and family allowances for all children.

In 1865, the first women's suffrage society was formed in Manchester, and the movement spread to London, Birmingham and Bristol. In 1889 the **Women's Franchise League** was formed. Among the most prominent members of the league was **Emmeline Pankhurst** (1858–1928).

OUR LEAGUE TOOK UP THE RIGHTS OF MARRIED WOMEN, A GROUP PREVIOUSLY IGNORED BY THE WOMEN'S MOVEMENT.

IN FACT, EVEN IN THE CAMPAIGN FOR SUFFRAGE, MARRIED WOMEN HAD PREVIOUSLY BEEN EXCLUDED FROM THE AGENDA.

# The Woman's Social and Political Union

Emmeline Pankhurst was born in Manchester and studied at the École Normale in Paris. She married a barrister who advocated equality for women, and in 1903 she founded the **Woman's Social and Political Union** (WSPU), an organization dedicated to obtaining the vote for women in Britain. She held public meetings in London and led protest marches to the House of Commons.

BUT THERE WAS LITTLE CHANGE IN LEGISLATION, SO I RESORTED TO CIVIL DISOBEDIENCE AND DEFIANTLY BROKE THE LAW IN ORDER TO ATTRACT ATTENTION TO THE UNION.

The WSPU became militant, smashing windows and burning unoccupied buildings; they heckled political meetings and chained themselves to railings.

# Militant Suffragettes

By 1911, suffrage had still not been achieved. The suffragettes became more violent and committed arson, cut telephone wires and burned phone boxes, slashed paintings in public galleries and threw bombs at commercial buildings. Jailed for the first time in 1908, Pankhurst continued her protest through a hunger strike. She undertook ten hunger strikes during subsequent arrests, and was released and then rearrested depending on her health. She was assisted by her three daughters, who were as energetic and dedicated as she was.

Speaking in her defence in court, she asserted:

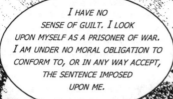

> *I HAVE NO SENSE OF GUILT. I LOOK UPON MYSELF AS A PRISONER OF WAR. I AM UNDER NO MORAL OBLIGATION TO CONFORM TO, OR IN ANY WAY ACCEPT, THE SENTENCE IMPOSED UPON ME.*

During the First World War, the government released all suffragettes from prison and offered the WSPU £2,000 in return for the end of their militant activities and their participation in the war effort. Pankhurst organized a demonstration in London calling on trade unions to allow women access to professions reserved for men. Banners were carried with slogans such as:

WE DEMAND THE RIGHT TO SERVE

FOR MEN MUST FIGHT AND WOMEN MUST WORK

LET NONE BE KAISER'S CAT'S PAWS

FOR KING, FOR COUNTRY, FOR FREEDOM

# Women's Suffrage in Australia

The Australian pioneer feminist **Vida Goldstein** (1869–1949) stands out as a significant figure in the history of female suffrage. In 1899, after starting a career as headteacher of a school she founded at St Kilda, Melbourne, she decided to devote her social activities to the women's suffrage movement and campaigned for the Queen Victoria Hospital for women.

Goldstein travelled to Britain and the US to participate in various conventions, and in 1902 she attended the Women's Suffrage Conference in Washington DC.

Goldstein was a social reformer and, in 1903, became the first Australian woman candidate to stand for a national parliament in the British Empire. Although her bid for a seat in the Senate was unsuccessful, she stood for parliament (again unsuccessfully) for five consecutive years (1910–17).

*I FOUNDED A MONTHLY FEMINIST NEWSPAPER, WOMEN'S SPHERE (1899–1905), AND THEN WOMAN VOTER IN 1909.*

*AND I WROTE IN SUPPORT OF BIRTH CONTROL AND EQUAL NATURALIZATION LAWS.*

Goldstein was also a pacifist. During the First World War, she chaired the Peace Alliance and formed the Women's Peace Army, to which she recruited the British suffragette Adela Pankhurst.

# Suffrage Gains Momentum

The fight to achieve full voting rights for women was slow and at times violent. But achieving suffrage was a milestone in the history of feminism.

**1892**  New Zealand is the first country to grant women's suffrage; women vote in the 1902 elections, sparking a wave of suffrage around the world

**1902**  Australian women achieve the right to vote

**1906**  Finland extends the vote to women

**1913**  Norway

**1915**  Denmark

**1917**  The Netherlands and the Union of Soviet Socialist Republics

**1918**  British women over the age of 30 gain the vote. Canada and Luxembourg

**1919**  Austria, Czechoslovakia, Germany, Poland and Sweden. Belgium grants partial vote

**1920**  US women gain the vote

**1928**  British women 21 years and older are extended full voting rights

**1929**  Ecuador

**1934**  Turkey grants suffrage to women

**1944**  France

**1946**  Women gain the vote in Japan

**1947**  China and Argentina

**1948**  women vote in South Korea; full vote in Belgium

**1955**  educated women can vote in Iraq

**1958**  voting opened to Muslim women in Algeria

**1963**  Libya

**1971**  in Switzerland, women vote in Federal elections

**1990**  women vote in all Swiss cantons

By the 1980s, women could vote almost anywhere around the world except for a few Muslim countries. In Kuwait, for example, women are still not allowed to vote.

# Against Suffrage

Once the vote was won in Britain and the US, few feminists remained active. Those who did fought for contraceptive rights, abortion law reform and the chance to be admitted to certain professions.

What must be noted here is that the fight to achieve suffrage was often accompanied by similar protest against it. One notable example from 1913 is that of Grace Duffield Goodwin.

$ACRED $MOTHERHOOD

*AMERICAN WOMEN AS A WHOLE ARE SUFFERING UNDER NO WRONGS WHICH NEED FOR THEIR REDRESS THE VIOLENT OVERTURNING OF THE ENTIRE POLITICAL MACHINERY OF THE NATION.*

GRACE DUFFIELD GOODWIN

She cautioned that the pursuit of suffrage would threaten women's domesticity, motherhood and the entire social order.

73

# The First Backlash

Feminist activity at the beginning of the 20th century caused serious controversy which translated into a number of outspoken and vehement publications attacking "feminists" for being immoral, bad mothers and lesbians.

WOMEN'S DESIRE TO PARTICIPATE IN POLITICS AND TO ACHIEVE ECONOMIC INDEPENDENCE AND PERSONAL AUTONOMY IS EXPLAINED AS A SYMPTOM OF ABNORMAL SEXUALITY AND PERVERSE DESIRE.

THIS UNNATURAL BEHAVIOUR IS A SIGN OF HOMOSEXUALITY, OF WOMEN WANTING TO PERFORM MASCULINE ROLES.

In 1911, the English writer Edward Carpenter described feminist women as "mannish in temperament", with poor maternal instinct, and lesbian.

# Feminism = Lesbianism?

In 1901, the American psychiatrist William Lee Howard wrote a novel entitled *The Perverts*, which equated feminism with lesbianism and degenerate morality.

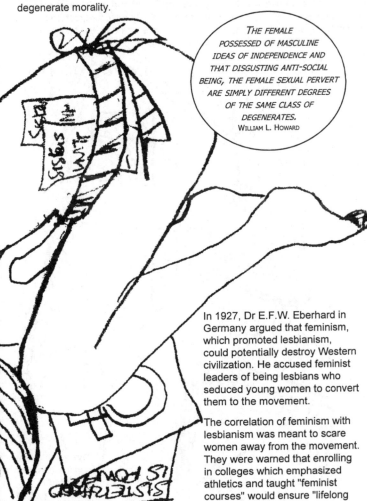

> *THE FEMALE POSSESSED OF MASCULINE IDEAS OF INDEPENDENCE AND THAT DISGUSTING ANTI-SOCIAL BEING, THE FEMALE SEXUAL PERVERT ARE SIMPLY DIFFERENT DEGREES OF THE SAME CLASS OF DEGENERATES.*
> WILLIAM L. HOWARD

In 1927, Dr E.F.W. Eberhard in Germany argued that feminism, which promoted lesbianism, could potentially destroy Western civilization. He accused feminist leaders of being lesbians who seduced young women to convert them to the movement.

The correlation of feminism with lesbianism was meant to scare women away from the movement. They were warned that enrolling in colleges which emphasized athletics and taught "feminist courses" would ensure "lifelong homosexuality".

## Educated but Under-employed

Some critics argue that feminism died in the US in the 1920s because of complacency following the achieving of suffrage for women. This is the period that Betty Friedan would later dub the era of "the feminine mystique" (see pages 90–4). Women were increasingly highly educated, achieving university-level qualifications, and although more women were employed, their position within the labour force was declining.

WHILE MEN ARE ABLE TO TAKE ON PROFESSIONS TRADITIONALLY ASSOCIATED WITH WOMEN, SUCH AS TEACHING AND SOCIAL WORK ...

... THE REVERSE IS NOT TRUE FOR WOMEN.

The result was a surplus of highly educated, under-employed women.

## The Lost Sex

Anti-feminist propaganda undermined efforts to promote women's rights and culminated in the publication of the bestseller *Modern Woman: The Lost Sex* in 1942, which emphasized the need for women to return to the home and give up their high-paying jobs in war production. The "lost" women were the independent ones interested in science, art and politics, and those engaged in careers beyond their domestic sphere. The book described feminism as an "expression of emotional illness, of neurosis … at its core a deep illness".

Some titles taken from women's magazines in 1949:

FEMININITY BEGINS AT HOME
HAVE BABIES WHILE YOU'RE YOUNG
HOW TO SNARE A MAN
SHOULD I STOP WORK WHEN WE MARRY?
ARE YOU TRAINING YOUR DAUGHTER TO BE A WIFE?
DO WOMEN HAVE TO TALK SO MUCH?
COOKING TO ME IS POETRY
WHY GIs PREFER THOSE GERMAN GIRLS

# Virginia Woolf

Among the best-known of the novelists and feminist writers who questioned women's contribution to social and political life was **Virginia Woolf** (1882–1941). Woolf was married to the political journalist Leonard Woolf, with whom she founded the Hogarth Press, which published relatively unknown writers such as Katherine Mansfield, T.S. Eliot and E.M. Forster. Hogarth also made the first English translations of Freud's psychoanalytic theories.

KATHERINE MANSFIELD

WOOLF IS A MODERNIST WRITER WHO EXPLORES THE LIMITATIONS OF CONVENTIONAL NARRATIVE GENRES AND SETS OUT TO CREATE A FORM OF FEMALE SELF-EXPRESSION.

I USE STREAM OF CONSCIOUSNESS IN MY NARRATIVES BECAUSE I WANT TO DESCRIBE THE ATOMS AS THEY FALL UPON THE MIND IN THE ORDER IN WHICH THEY FALL.

VIRGINIA WOOLF

# A Room of One's Own

Woolf was invited to deliver a series of lectures at Newnham and Girton, the only colleges for women at Cambridge University at that time. *A Room of One's Own* (1929) consists of an edited version of her lectures on "Women and Fiction", and was first published by Hogarth Press in 1929.

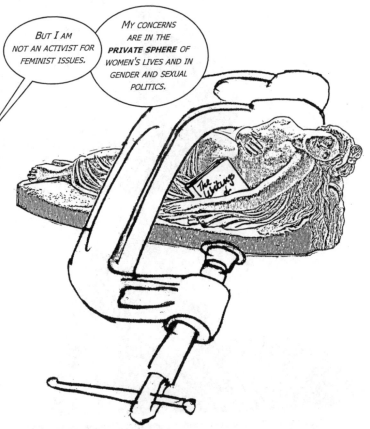

In *A Room of One's Own*, she explored the cultural and economic constraints on female creativity and pondered the historical and political obstacles which have hampered the establishing of a female literary tradition.

## Guineas and Locks

Woolf's best-known assertion is that in order for a woman to be creative, she needs a steady income of £500 a year and a room of her own "guineas and locks". In a later essay entitled "Professions for Women" she specifically identified two issues hindering female creativity:

In *Three Guineas* (1938) she attempted to construct a female identity which would transcend national and political boundaries. She addressed the social role of middle class "daughters of educated men" and commented on their education, their career prospects and their potential to contribute to national culture, from which they had been historically excluded.

# "I have no country ..."

Although Woolf is often regarded as a feminist literary critic rather than a social activist, her writing often displays acute awareness of discrimination and social marginalization. *A Room of One's Own* is littered with examples of situations where women are actively barred from social and cultural media such as libraries, universities and exclusively male eating places. In many ways, her writing becomes more relevant to later feminists who pursued **consciousness-raising** during the second wave of feminist activity.

AS A WOMAN I HAVE NO COUNTRY. AS A WOMAN I WANT NO COUNTRY. AS A WOMAN MY COUNTRY IS THE WHOLE WORLD.

Her ideas on the need for establishing a female literary tradition were later taken up by the **gynocritics** (see pages 124–5).

81

# Simone de Beauvoir

**Simone de Beauvoir**'s *The Second Sex* (1949) ushered in a new era of thinking about woman's position in society, and it has become a classic of feminist philosophy. De Beauvoir (1908–86) offered a new understanding of social relations between men and women. Her interpretation of the social construction of femininity as **Other** paved the way for the theoretical discussions of the second wave.

# Existence Precedes Essence

De Beauvoir explained subjectivity (our sense of Self) through exis
philosophy. Existentialism proposes that one exists first, and through
one's acts, one becomes something. She reasoned that an individual has
absolute control over their fate, and neither society nor organized religion
should limit our freedom to live authentically.

WE CONSTRUCT
OUR SENSE OF SELF IN
RELATION TO SOMETHING WHICH
IS NOT "OUR SELF" —
AN OTHER.

But since men have claimed the category of Self, of Subject, for
themselves, woman is relegated to the status of Other. Consequently,
the category of woman has no substance except as an extension of male
fantasy and fears.

Since all cultural representations of the world around us have been produced by men, women read themselves in terms of masculine definitions and "dream through the dreams of men". Thus woman is required to accept her status of Other, "make herself object" and "renounce her autonomy".

## Milestones of Second Wave Feminism

**1960**   First oral contraceptive developed by American scientists is approved for use

**1963**   John F. Kennedy creates the Commission on the Status of Women which will expose discrimination against women in employment
Betty Friedan, *The Feminine Mystique*

**1966**   National Organization for Women (NOW)

**1968**   Student revolution in France
Miss America protests

**1970**   Germaine Greer, *The Female Eunuch*
Shulamith Firestone, *The Dialectic of Sex*
Kate Millet, *Sexual Politics*

**1971**   *Ms* magazine is founded by Gloria Steinem

**1972**   Spare Rib is launched in the UK (until 1993)

**1974**   Ann Oakley, *Women's Work*

**1976**   Adrienne Rich, *Of Woman Born*
Dorothy Dinnerstein, *The Mermaid and the Minotaur*

**1978**   Mary Daly, *Gyn/Ecology*
Nancy Chodorow, *The Reproduction of Mothering*

**1981**   bell hooks, *Ain't I a Woman?*

**1982**   Combahee River Collective issue their statement

**1983**   Alice Walker, *In Search of Our Mother's Garden: Womanist Prose*

**1991**   Naomi Wolf, *The Beauty Myth*
Susan Faludi, *Backlash*

**1994**   Violence Against Women Act (US)

ILLUSTRATION BY OSCAR ZARATE

In England, 1981, women activists protested at the government's decision to site 96 Cruise missiles on Greenham Common, Berkshire. They set up the "Greenham Common Women's Peace Camp" outside the RAF base. The protest lasted for nineteen years, publicising the case against nuclear warfare.

# Second Wave Feminism

**Second wave feminists** adopted and adapted De Beauvoir's reasoning that women's oppression lay in their socially constructed status of Other to men. The term "second wave" was coined by Marsha Lear to describe the increase in feminist activity in America, Britain and Europe from the late 1960s onwards.

*TWO POLITICAL MOVEMENTS SHAPED THE SECOND WAVE: THE **WOMEN'S RIGHTS MOVEMENT** (WRM) AND THE **WOMEN'S LIBERATION MOVEMENT** (WLM).*

*THE WRM WAS COMPOSED LARGELY OF PROFESSIONAL WOMEN WHO CAMPAIGNED TO END DISCRIMINATION AGAINST WOMEN AT WORK.*

*THIS MOVEMENT ALSO ATTRACTED MIDDLE-CLASS HOUSEWIVES WHO FELT DISSATISFIED WITH THEIR DOMESTIC CONFINEMENT AND WHO WANTED TO PARTICIPATE IN THE LABOUR FORCE.*

# The Women's Liberation Movement

The WLM emerged out of the New Left of the WRM in the late 1960s. In the US, it came as a result of civil rights activism and anti-Vietnam campaigning. The WLM provided **theoretical** solutions to women's oppression, whereas the WRM was the more **practical** and socially driven movement.

# The Personal is Political

The slogan "the personal is political" referred to the fact that every aspect of a woman's private life is affected by and can itself affect the political situation.

In Britain, where working-class socialism predominated, women workers at the Ford car plant went on strike to protest against gaps in pay. More recent feminists have challenged early interpretations of the slogan and have invited women to separate the personal from the political.

## The Seven Demands of the WLM

By the mid-20th century, the Women's Liberation Movement had developed clear objectives and was campaigning to achieve:

1. Equal pay for men and women
2. Equal education and job opportunities
3. Free 24-hour nurseries
4. Free contraception and abortion on demand
5. Financial and legal independence
6. An end to discrimination against lesbians and a woman's right to define her sexuality
7. Freedom from intimidation by threat or use of violence and an end to male aggression and dominance

# Betty Friedan

In 1963, **Betty Friedan** (1921–2006) published the best-selling *The Feminine Mystique*, which heralded feminism's second wave. The title refers to the idealization of traditional roles ascribed to women (as wives and mothers) which is interpreted as a means of keeping women subordinate to men.

SHE CHALLENGES THE LONG-HELD NOTIONS THAT WOMEN CAN FIND FULFILMENT ONLY IN DOMESTIC ROLES.

I INVITE WOMEN TO SEE THEMSELVES AS INDIVIDUALS WITH A POTENTIAL FOR ACHIEVING THEIR DREAMS.

"OCCUPATION: HOUSEWIFE" IS A PHRASE SHE PARTICULARLY OBJECTS TO.

the problem that has no name

# The Feminine Mystique

"The feminine mystique says that the highest value and the only commitment for women is the fulfilment of their own femininity ...

"... it says that this femininity is so mysterious and intuitive and close to the creation and origin of life that man-made science may never be able to understand it.

"The mistake, says the mystique, the root of women's troubles in the past is that women envied men, instead of accepting their own nature, which can find fulfilment only in sexual passivity, male domination, and nurturing maternal love."

Friedan was instrumental in consciousness-raising, and appealed to women because, unlike de Beauvoir's philosophical *Second Sex*, her book was based on her personal experiences and those of real women (it was based on questionnaires she distributed to her former classmates).

## Motherhood Before Career?

Friedan began her working career as a journalist. She was dismissed when she became pregnant, and it was this incident which made her aware of social discrimination against professional women. She believed that since American society was predicated upon the pursuit of the American Dream, all that was needed for women's liberation was a national programme of education which would lead to fulfilling work and would liberate both sexes.

Friedan maintained that if women learned how to juggle their various domestic duties, they would find the time and energy to engage in professional careers. This would ensure them private and public satisfaction.

There are many problematic issues about Friedan's argument: She did not identify the source of women's oppression, nor did she take into consideration women's varied access to education. Friedan, like de Beauvoir, focused solely on the experience of middle-class, heterosexual, white women. Both critics tended to blame women themselves for their subordinate position and failed to acknowledge the need for society to change in order to accommodate women's changing lives.

Friedan was a formidable activist, however.

*I WAS RESPONSIBLE FOR FOUNDING THE **NATIONAL ORGANIZATION FOR WOMEN** (NOW) IN 1966 ...*

*... AND FOR ORGANIZING THE **NATIONAL WOMEN'S POLITICAL CAUCUS** IN 1971 AND THE **INTERNATIONAL FEMINIST CONGRESS** IN 1973.*

*AND I STARTED THE **FIRST WOMEN'S BANK** IN 1973.*

WOMEN NEED CONSTITUTIONAL EQUALITY N.O.W.

**NOW**
NATIONAL
ORGANIZATION
FOR WOMEN

# The Feminist Mystique

In her later publication *The Second Stage* (1981), she detailed the obstacles facing women who attempt to combine marriage and a career.

IN OUR REACTION AGAINST THE **FEMININE** MYSTIQUE, WHICH DEFINED WOMEN SOLELY IN TERMS OF THEIR RELATION TO MEN AS WIVES, MOTHERS AND HOMEMAKERS, WE SOMETIMES SEEMED TO FALL INTO A **FEMINIST** MYSTIQUE ...

... WHICH DENIED THAT CORE OF WOMEN'S PERSONHOOD THAT IS FULFIL THROUGH LOVE, NURTURE HOME.

These Superwomen of the 1980s attempted to achieve the impossible task of being both "woman" at home and "man" at work. Friedan claimed that in order to resolve their dilemma, the women's movement should be restarted, and this time men should be involved in order to change public values, leadership styles, and institutional structures.

# C-R and Rap

Feminist activists of the 1970s understood the need to make their case heard by more people, but they also aimed at making the movement for women's liberation more inclusive and representative. In the US, **consciousness-raising** (C-R) efforts took the shape of **rap groups** organized around the country.

Rap groups brought women from various backgrounds together in a social structure where they could interact and compare their common concerns. These groups educated their members about the politics of discrimination, altering their perceptions and conceptions of themselves in relation to society. The groups were characterized by their unstructured approach.

# Varieties of Feminisms

Since the 1960s, a variety of feminist perspectives on women's lives has given rise to a number of feminist positions.

**Lesbian feminism** warns that compulsory heterosexuality perpetuates women's sexual oppression. In 1955, a group of lesbian feminist activists in San Francisco formed Daughters of Bilitis, taking their name from Pierre Louÿs' Sapphic love poetry *Chansons de Bilitis*. In Britain in the late 1970s, the Leeds Revolutionary Feminists made the "case against heterosexuality".

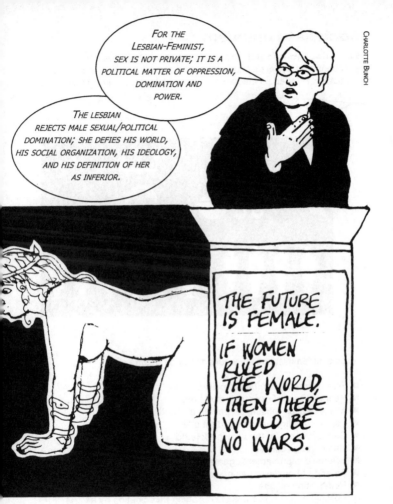

FOR THE LESBIAN-FEMINIST, SEX IS NOT PRIVATE; IT IS A POLITICAL MATTER OF OPPRESSION, DOMINATION AND POWER.

THE LESBIAN REJECTS MALE SEXUAL/POLITICAL DOMINATION; SHE DEFIES HIS WORLD, HIS SOCIAL ORGANIZATION, HIS IDEOLOGY, AND HIS DEFINITION OF HER AS INFERIOR.

CHARLOTTE BUNCH

THE FUTURE IS FEMALE.

IF WOMEN RULED THE WORLD, THEN THERE WOULD BE NO WARS.

**Cultural feminists** believe that women have been separated from each other and convinced of their inferiority. The lesbian is the only woman who can realize her full potential.

97

# Socialist Feminism

**Socialist feminism** asserts that women are held back by lack of education and social discrimination, and argues that a change in public attitudes is needed so that women can be integrated into all levels of society.

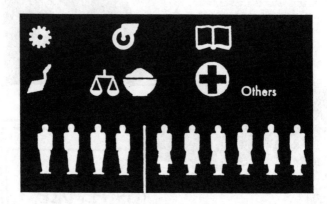

A socialist feminist society would demand /ensure:

- Free, humane, competent medical care
- Peoples' control over their own bodies
- Availability of housing for private and collective use
- Varied, nutritious and abundant diet
- Social respect for the work people do
- Democratic councils
- Scientific improvements geared towards the improvement of human life
- An end of housework as private unpaid labour
- Redefinition of jobs
- Political and civil liberties encouraging participation by all
- Disarming of and community control of police
- Social responsibility for the raising of children
- Free, public quality education
- Freedom to define social and sexual relationships
- A popular culture which enhances self-respect and respect of others
- Support for internal development and self-determination for countries around the world.

Socialist feminists saw great potential in uniting women into bonds of **sisterhood** which would allow for a revolutionary seizing of power. They developed a tripartite strategy.

1) Win real concrete reforms that meet women's needs
2) Give women a sense of their own power
3) Alter the relations of power

*PARTICIPATION IN RAP GROUPS MIGHT LEAD WOMEN TO A DEAD END IF NOT COUPLED WITH ACTION AND SUPPORTED BY A CLEAR SENSE OF IDEOLOGY.*

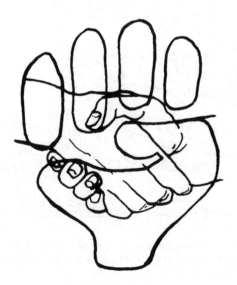

# Traditional Marxist Feminism

For Marxist feminists, the division of labour and lack of support for working mothers defines women by their domestic responsibilities and excludes them from productive labour.

Marxist feminists oppose the Women's Liberation Movement's emphasis on achieving goals relevant only to middle-class women (see Shulamith Firestone, pages 114–16).

# Radical Feminism

**Radical feminism** sees itself as revolutionary. It maintains that women's emancipation is not enough, and argues that women are still oppressed and exploited. The only way to "free" them is by opposing patriarchy and marriage. Radical feminists question every aspect of women's lives.

*To be a radical feminist involves finding new ways of doing things which were previously accepted as normal/given/ standard/acceptable.*

Gail Chester

Radical feminism also entails re-thinking language, which is male-defined and expresses male-dominated values. Hence the radicals argue for revising language so that male definitions of the world can be appropriated to reflect women's experience and participation in it.

101

Radical feminists emphasize the need to practise consciousness-raising as a revolutionary tool. According to Gail Chester...

**Female supremacists** believe that women are biologically and morally superior, although men hold power by force of arms.

> WOMEN MUST WAGE WAR AGAINST THE PHALLOCRATS!

**Humanist feminists** argue that both men and women are being forced into socially-constructed masculine and feminine roles which hinder the development of their authentic selves.

WOMEN UNITE!

TALK ABOUT WHAT WE...
DO WHAT WE...

> SOCIETY MUST TREAT ALL PEOPLE AS EQUAL BY ESTABLISHING COMMUNAL GROUPS, SHORTENING WORKING HOURS AND ENCOURAGING EQUAL CHILDCARE RESPONSIBILITIES.

Indoch...
Racism
Working Conditions
etc.

Guillermo

ALEXANDRA KOLLONTAI

**ALEXANDRA KOLLONTAI** (1872–1952) WAS A MARXIST FEMINIST ACTIVIST. SHE FOUGHT FOR THE RIGHTS OF WOMEN WORKERS IN RUSSIA AND ENCOURAGED THEM TO CHALLENGE THEIR EMPLOYERS.

# Ecofeminism

**Ecofeminism** encompasses a variety of feminist perspectives.
**Françoise d'Eubonne** coined the term in 1974 and it has since been used to refer to a range of ideas on ecological feminist practices. These ideas reflect different understandings of the nature of, and solution to, current environmental problems.

In spite of their diverse approaches, ecofeminists agree that the destruction of the natural environment is politically analogous to the continued domination of women.

OUR METHODOLOGY THUS INVOLVES FINDING WAYS IN WHICH THE OPPRESSION OF WOMEN CAN BE CORRELATED TO THE DESTRUCTION OF THE ENVIRONMENT — AND COMING UP WITH SOLUTIONS TO BOTH PROBLEMS.

Ecofeminists often resort to a critique of **technology**.

*TECHNOLOGY ALLOWS THE INVASION AND APPROPRIATION OF NATURE AND OF THE FEMALE BODY.*

*ECOFEMINISM IS SOMETIMES SEEN AS AN **ESSENTIALIST** FORM OF THINKING IN ITS ATTEMPTS TO EQUATE WOMEN WITH NATURE.*

While technology is regarded by some ecofeminists as a tool of patriarchal oppression, another branch of ecofeminists finds that technological advances offer utopian possibilities for women, since they liberate them from their traditional roles as domestic workers.

# Psychoanalytic Feminism

In 1972 **Phyllis Chesler** published *Women and Madness*, which detailed her observations of women patients at a mental institution in New York.

*PSYCHOANALYSIS REGARDS MADNESS AS A NORMATIVE CHARACTERISTIC OF FEMININITY.*

*FROM THIS POINT ONWARDS, THERE WAS A DEBATE OVER THE EXTENT TO WHICH FREUDIAN PSYCHOANALYSIS CAN BE USED TO EXPLAIN WOMEN'S LIVES.*

PHYLLIS CHESLER

Many critics went on to use or denounce Freud for his theories on femininity and gender socialization, but it wasn't until **Juliet Mitchell**'s *Feminism and Psychoanalysis* (1974) that feminist theorists began to see "psychoanalysis not as a recommendation for a patriarchal society but an analysis of one".

(See pages 126–32 for more on psychoanalysis and feminism.)

# Postfeminism

In 1968 in France, the Women's Liberation Movement (known as MLF) split into two factions. One group of feminists maintained that achieving *equality* with men should remain the aim of the movement, while another argued for the importance of maintaining *difference* between men and women.

This second branch of the MLF, the **postfeminist** faction, encompasses psychoanalytic critics such as **Julia Kristeva** and **Hélène Cixous**.

*WE EMPHASIZE THE NEED TO RECOGNIZE THE FUNDAMENTAL DIFFERENCES BETWEEN MEN AND WOMEN IN ORDER TO APPRECIATE WOMEN'S MULTIPLE SUBJECTIVITIES.*

Julia Kristeva

# Protest and Revolt

One of the goals of feminist activism is to militate against any form of **female objectification**. Beauty contests are particularly contentious because they entail the parading of scantily-dressed young women and judging them according to conventional – and controversial – standards of femininity.

On 7 September 1968, American feminists staged a protest against the Miss America contest because it was deemed exploitative and demeaning to women.

WE NOMINATED A SHEEP FOR MISS AMERICA, AND THREW SYMBOLS OF PATRIARCHAL OPPRESSION SUCH AS BRAS, GIRDLES, FALSE EYELASHES, BRASSIERES AND HIGH HEELS INTO A "FREEDOM TRASHCAN".

Flyers advertising the protest invited women to march into Atlantic City on the day and bring any type of "woman-garbage" including issues of *Cosmopolitan*, *Ladies' Home Journal* and *Family Circle* to be burned. The protest, which announced the boycott of all commercial products related to the pageant, organized a Women's Liberation Rally at midnight when Miss America would be crowned on live television.

Although they specifically declared that no heavy disruptive tactics would be used, the protesters expressed their refusal to cooperate with policemen.

This was an ironic statement with a political message of its own, since in Atlantic City women police officers were not allowed to make any arrests.

The protest was not granted a fire licence on the day, so the Freedom Trashcan was never lit. However, this incident started rumours of "bra burning" in the press.

WE ISSUED A MANIFESTO HIGHLIGHTING TEN POINTS OF CONTENTION. WE PROTESTED AGAINST:

- The degrading Mindless-Boob-Girlie Symbol
- Racism with Roses (since its inception in 1921, all Miss America winners had been white)
- Miss America as Military Death Mascot (one of the beauty queen's duties was to do a cheer-leading tour of American forces abroad)
- The Consumer Con-game
- Competition rigged and unrigged
- The Woman as Pop Culture Obsolescent Theme (spindle, mutilate and then discard tomorrow)
- The Unbeatable Madonna-Whore Combination
- The Irrelevant Crown on the Throne of Mediocrity
- Miss America as Dream Equivalent to —? (Boys become President, girls beauty queens)

- Miss America as Big Sister Watching You (as oppressive role model)

# A Black Miss America

Although beauty pageants continued to be held, they caused regular controversy. In 1983, **Vanessa Williams** made history by becoming the first black woman ever to be crowned Miss America. A year later, she was to make history again when she was obliged to resign the title after the publication of explicit photos of her in *Penthouse* magazine. A number of prominent public figures supported her, including feminist activists Gloria Steinem and Susan Brownmiller and black politicians Jesse Jackson and Benjamin Hooks.

# Germaine Greer

**Germaine Greer** (b. 1939) has always been a controversial feminist figure. Since 1970, when her first publication *The Female Eunuch* became a bestseller, she has become known as a public figure and a spokesperson for the movement.

*The Female Eunuch* was a revolutionary work which criticized traditional family structures and the mechanism of the nuclear family, which Greer perceived as the source of women's disempowerment.

*HETEROSEXUALITY IS A FORM OF OPPRESSION, CONDITIONING WOMEN TO CONFORM TO THEIR SOCIETY'S EXPECTATIONS OF FEMININITY AND ENCOURAGING THEM TO BELIEVE THAT THEIR VALUE DEPENDS ON THEIR APPEAL TO MEN.*

GERMAINE GREER

Greer also criticized the workplace, where women are under pressure to please their male superiors in the same way as they do in their marriages. On this subject, the magazine *Vogue* quoted her saying:

Greer championed sexual liberation as a means of freeing sexual activity from the confines of patriarchal institutions.

However, in 1984 Greer published *Sex and Destiny*, another controversial text which contradicted *The Female Eunuch* by emphasizing chastity as the best form of contraception. Greer invited her audience to see the menopause as a liberatory experience.

# Shulamith Firestone

*The Dialectic of Sex* was published in 1970. **Shulamith Firestone** (b. 1945) believed that women's capacity for reproduction was the source of their oppression. Therefore in order to eradicate social inequality, a **biological revolution** is needed.

*ARTIFICIAL REPRODUCTION IS THE GATEWAY TO WOMEN'S LIBERATION.*

*IF WOMEN WERE NOT REQUIRED TO GO THROUGH PREGNANCY AND THE BARBARIC ACT OF CHILDBIRTH, THEN THEY WOULD ASSUME CONTROL OVER THEIR REPRODUCTIVE FUNCTIONS.*

An egalitarian society, she argued, could be achieved only through an **androgynous** system whereby it "no longer matters culturally" who possesses the womb. Under this system, the traditional structure of the family which ascribed clear sexual roles to each gender would dissolve, as heterosexuality would no longer be compulsory and women would be freed from their domestic confinement.

# Reproduction, not Production

Firestone revised Marx and Engels' theories of history, which overlooked women's exclusion from society.

*IN MY VERSION OF HISTORY, **SEX CLASS**, RATHER THAN ECONOMIC CLASS, IS THE CENTRAL CONCEPT.*

*I DISTINGUISH BETWEEN THE CLASS OF MEN AND THE CLASS OF WOMEN.*

SHULAMITH FIRESTONE

This distinction allowed her to examine **reproduction** rather than production as the driving force in history. Women should seize control over the means of reproduction in order to eliminate sex class discrimination. This can be achieved through wider access to contraception, sterilization and abortion.

# Consuming for Capitalism

Firestone explained that the biological family based on sex class discrimination benefits capitalism by making possible the confinement of women to the domestic sphere and enabling men to control the public sphere.

> AS UNPAID HOUSE WORKERS, WOMEN, AND THEIR CHILDREN, BECOME CONSUMERS IN SUPPORT OF THE CAPITALIST ECONOMY.

Capitalism is thus predicated upon the distinctions of woman-as-reproducer and man-as-producer. However, once women are freed from the responsibility to reproduce, they can participate in the workplace and achieve economic and personal independence.

# Kate Millet

**Kate Millet**'s *Sexual Politics* (1970) was another radical feminist text which explained the roots of women's oppression in terms of patriarchy's **sex/gender** system. Millet (b. 1934) insisted that sex is political because the relationship between males and females underlies all **power relations**.

BIOLOGICAL SEX IS NATURAL ... GENDER IS CULTURALLY CONSTRUCTED ... FEMININITY IS CULTURALLY DEFINED BASED ON SOCIETY'S UNDERSTANDING OF GENDER.

SOCIAL CASTE SUPERSEDES ALL OTHER FORMS OF INEGALITARIANISM: RACIAL, POLITICAL, OR ECONOMIC.

UNLESS THE CLINGING TO MALE SUPREMACY AS A BIRTHRIGHT IS FINALLY FORGONE, ALL SYSTEMS OF OPPRESSION WILL CONTINUE TO FUNCTION SIMPLY BY VIRTUE OF THEIR LOGICAL AND EMOTIONAL MANDATE IN THE PRIMARY HUMAN SITUATION.

KATE MILLET

# The Sex/Gender Hierarchy

Patriarchy is responsible for constructing a social system which ascribes a particular **sexual status**, **role** and **temperament** for each gender, hence ensuring the sex/gender hierarchy. As a result, "masculine" traits are attributed to dominant social roles while "feminine" is associated with submission and dependence.

# Misogyny in Literature

Millet looked to literature for examples of misogyny. She isolated the trio of **D.H. Lawrence**, **Henry Miller** and **Norman Mailer** as the worst culprits.

*LITERATURE ACTS AS A FORM OF PROPAGANDA FOR PATRIARCHY, AND THESE AUTHORS IN PARTICULAR HAD REACTIONARY IDEAS WHICH EXPLICITLY GLORIFIED THE STEREOTYPING AND OBJECTIFICATION OF WOMEN.*

Millet observed that in spite of persistent patriarchal domination, women have always resisted and challenged oppression. She described the women of 1970 as determined to obliterate the sex/gender system and to create a new, androgynous society in which men and women lead equal lives.

# Ann Oakley

Similarly to Firestone, **Ann Oakley** (b. 1944) made the case *against* biological motherhood. In *Women's Work* (1974) she challenged the "**myth of biological motherhood**" which is based on three assumptions:

> *THAT ALL WOMEN NEED TO BE MOTHERS, ALL MOTHERS NEED THEIR CHILDREN, ALL CHILDREN NEED THEIR MOTHERS.*

She systematically countered these assumptions by arguing that:

**1.** Women's need to be mothers is artificially instilled in them during socialization – when the mother teaches the daughter society's expectations of her – and is not an essential or natural part of their existence.

**2.** The belief that mothers need their children is based on the fallacy of a **maternal instinct** which must be satisfied or else the woman will become frustrated. Oakley refutes the idea that women are instinctively drawn to their children and asserts that mothers are not born, they are made.

**3.** The myth of biological motherhood is manifested most prominently in the assumption that all children need their mothers, which is itself based on erroneous reasoning.

## Subject Women

In 1981, Oakley published *Subject Women*, which evaluated the progress of the feminist movement. Oakley examined the legal, political, social and economic situation of women and assessed the degree to which their participation in society has affected their status of "second sex".

MEN, IN THE GUISE OF HUSBANDS, FATHERS AND BREADWINNERS, AND CAPITALISM, IN THE SENSE OF A MODE OF PRODUCTION THAT GIVES RISE TO A CERTAIN DIVISION OF CLASS INTERESTS, CAN BE HELD RESPONSIBLE FOR THE HABIT OF ACCORDING WOMEN A SECOND-CLASS STATUS.

Oakley reasoned that because "men are individualized" and capitalism is abstract, men have been more immediately blameable. Yet she also concluded that it was impossible to generate a patriarchal model of society which would correspond to a universal experience of women's oppression.

Oakley provocatively suggested that although some social groups might have conspired against women, yet women have also conspired among themselves and discriminated against their own kind. She advocated a more active engagement of feminists in the sociological aspects of women's lives rather than confining their efforts to the elite domains of research and academia.

# Gynocriticism

In the 1970s, a decade which witnessed intense feminist activity on the political and sociological levels, feminist academics became actively engaged in challenging the Western literary canon.

THE WESTERN CANON REVOLVES AROUND LITERARY WORK ENDORSED BY PATRIARCHY, WRITTEN MOSTLY BY MEN.

**Elaine Showalter**'s *A Literature of their Own* (1977) attempted to establish a literary tradition which reflected the variety of women's experience of the world. It also claimed women writers as significant contributors to the corpus of Western literary writing.

Showalter divided female literary history into three phases.

THE **FEMININE** PHASE (1840–80), IN WHICH WRITING PRODUCED BY WOMEN **IMITATED** MAINSTREAM PUBLICATIONS BY MEN.

THE **FEMINIST** PHASE (1880–1920), IN WHICH WOMEN WRITERS **PROTESTED** AGAINST THEIR MARGINALIZATION.

THE **FEMALE** PHASE (1920 ONWARDS), WHEN WOMEN'S WRITING IS PREOCCUPIED WITH **SELF-DISCOVERY**.

ELAINE SHOWALTER

In 1979, Showalter coined the term "**gynocriticism**" to refer to a form of critical practice whereby the "psychodynamics of female creativity" is explored and recorded. Gynocriticism became associated with Anglo-American feminist literary criticism, and **Sandra M. Gilbert** and **Susan Gubar**'s *The Madwoman in the Attic* (1979) is one of its most influential works. It attempted to establish an Anglo-American literary tradition of women without referring to or incorporating male authors.

# Psychoanalysis and Feminist Thought

In the 1970s, many feminists such as Firestone, Friedan and Millet castigated Freud for his theory of **penis envy**, which claimed that a girl's perception of herself and all those like her is that of "inferior castrates". They argued that women's social status of powerless Other had little to do with biology (gender) and much to do with social constructs of femininity.

BETTY FRIEDAN

FREUD'S APHORISM "ANATOMY IS DESTINY" SIGNIFIES THAT A WOMAN'S REPRODUCTIVE ROLE, GENDER IDENTITY AND SEXUAL PREFERENCE ARE DETERMINED BY THE LACK OF PENIS.

CONSEQUENTLY ANY WOMAN WHO DOES NOT ACT ACCORDING TO WHAT BIOLOGY HAS DETERMINED FOR HER IS "ABNORMAL".

Friedan rejected Freud's over-emphasis on sexuality and argued that it was society's obsessive concern with the female body that discriminated against women. She promoted a focus on the socio-economic and cultural situations which determine women's fate, rather than their lack of a body part.

Yet feminist critics have never had a unified voice. Their strengths lie in the diversity of their perspectives.

THE POWER OF THE FATHER

*OPPOSING FRIEDAN, I ENDORSE FREUD'S EMPHASIS ON FEMALE SEXUALITY, BUT INTERPRET IT IN POLITICAL TERMS.*

*MY REJECTION OF FREUD IS DUE TO HIS LACK OF ATTENTION TO RELATIONSHIPS OF POWER WITHIN THE FAMILY AND HIS SEEMING OBLIVION TO THE POWER OF THE FATHER.*

SHULAMITH FIRESTONE

Yet a number of feminist critics found in Freudian psychoanalysis useful concepts which they adapted to their understanding of female sexuality and women's relationship to motherhood, as we'll see.

## "The Reproduction of Mothering"

**Dorothy Dinnerstein** and **Nancy Chodorow** are two feminist critics who used a psychoanalytic framework for analysing the complicated role that women as mothers play in society. They focused on the Freudian concept of the **pre-Oedipal stage** of psychosexual development – during which the infant is still attached to its mother – to show how sexuality and gender are constructed to give primacy to men over women.

WE ARE OPPOSED TO THE IDEA THAT MOTHERS ARE RESPONSIBLE FOR MOST OF THE PARENTING OF THEIR CHILDREN.

DUAL PARENTING IS A PRACTICE WHICH WOULD ENABLE CHILDREN TO SEE THEIR FATHERS AS **ACCESSIBLE** AND **FALLIBLE** CREATURES.

DOROTHY DINNERSTEIN

# Mermaids and Minotaurs

Dinnerstein re-interpreted the significance of the pre-Oedipal stage in her analysis of how culture's gender arrangements have influenced women and men's perception of themselves as **mermaids** and **minotaurs**.

*THE TREACHEROUS MERMAID, SEDUCTIVE AND IMPENETRABLE FEMALE REPRESENTATIVE OF THE DARK AND MAGIC UNDERWATER WORLD FROM WHICH OUR LIFE COMES AND IN WHICH WE CANNOT LIVE, LURES VOYAGERS TO THEIR DOOM.*

*THE FEARSOME MINOTAUR, GIGANTIC ETERNALLY INFANTILE OFFSPRING OF A MOTHER'S UNNATURAL LUST, MALE REPRESENTATIVE OF MINDLESS, GREEDY POWER, INSATIABLY DEVOURS LIVE HUMAN FLESH.*

Why are women mermaids and men minotaurs?

The answer lies in the pre-Oedipal stage when the infant boy develops conflicting feelings towards his mother's body, which he sees as the source of pleasure and pain. The grown-up man wants to avoid this dependence on the female body by controlling it. For her part, the girl deals with the power of the mother within her by seeking to be controlled by men. This results in a mis-shaped set of six gender arrangements which determine all human relations.

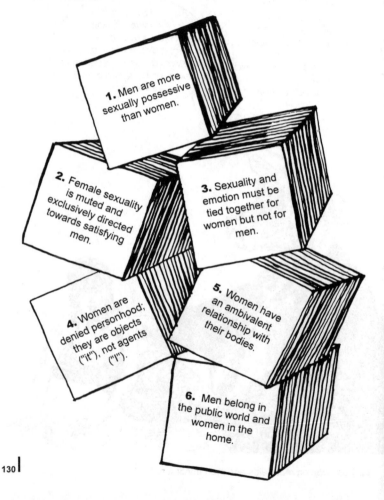

**1.** Men are more sexually possessive than women.

**2.** Female sexuality is muted and exclusively directed towards satisfying men.

**3.** Sexuality and emotion must be tied together for women but not for men.

**4.** Women are denied personhood; they are objects ("it"), not agents ("I").

**5.** Women have an ambivalent relationship with their bodies.

**6.** Men belong in the public world and women in the home.

# Separation from the Mother

Chodorow was less interested in sexual relationships and more attentive to asking why women decide to mother, even when social conditions do not force them into this role. Chodorow refuted Freud's suggestion that having children is a means for women to compensate for penis envy.

*I MAINTAIN THAT BOYS FIND THEIR SEPARATION FROM MOTHERS LESS TRAUMATIC THAN GIRLS BECAUSE IT ENABLES THEM TO BECOME MEN AND IDENTIFY WITH THEIR FATHERS.*

*GIRLS SUFFER FROM "PROLONGED SYMBIOSIS" AND "NARCISSISTIC OVER-IDENTIFICATION" BECAUSE THEY SEE THEMSELVES AS CONTINUOUS WITH THEIR MOTHERS.*

NANCY CHODOROW

The boy's separation from his mother engenders emotional deficiencies and the sense of a struggle for survival which prepares him for his public role as a competing male. In contrast, the girl who remains attached to her mother is able to empathize with others, forming warm and intimate relationships which hold the private domestic world together.

*IF CHILDREN WERE PARENTED BY THEIR MOTHER AND FATHER EQUALLY, THEN THESE ASYMMETRIES WOULD BE MINIMIZED.*

*GIRLS WOULD LEARN FROM THEIR FATHERS TO CONTROL THEIR EMPATHY WHILE BOYS WOULD LEARN TO STRIKE A BALANCE BETWEEN THEIR AUTONOMY AND EMOTIONAL EXPRESSION.*

# Adrienne Rich

**Adrienne Rich** (b. 1929) made the case for biological motherhood and argued against Firestone and Oakley's analyses.

In her book *Of Woman Born* (1976), Rich noted that women's experiences of pregnancy, childbirth and mothering are increasingly controlled by male doctors, who are replacing female midwives.

THIS CONTROL OVER WOMEN'S REPRODUCTION AND THEIR BODIES ENABLES THE PERPETUATION OF PATRIARCHAL PRINCIPLES WHICH DICTATE TO WOMEN WHEN TO EAT, SLEEP, EXERCISE, HAVE SEX, BREASTFEED, FEEL PLEASURE AND ENDURE PAIN.

Rich concluded that if women reclaimed control over their bodies during pregnancy and were able to perform motherhood without interference from male representatives of the patriarchal establishment, then they would become less alienated from their bodies, their spirits and the institution of motherhood.

As a feminist who identifies as a lesbian, Rich coined the term **"compulsory heterosexuality"** in 1980. She maintained that patriarchal society dictates that women must choose men as their sexual partners and perpetuates the ideology of the heterosexual romance. Consequently, lesbian sexuality is seen as deviant and transgressive.

*THE EMPHASIS ON THE PRIMACY OF THE MAN—WOMAN RELATIONSHIP PRECLUDES THE DEVELOPMENT OF ANY BONDS OF SISTERHOOD BETWEEN WOMEN.*

Rich expands the definition of lesbian relationships between women to include close ties of friendship and support. This has caused controversy within lesbian feminist groups, who insist that identification as a lesbian must encompass a woman's political and sexual practices.

# Gyn/Ecology

**Mary Daly** (b. 1928) is a radical feminist philosopher and theologian. In 1973 she published *God the Father*, in which she maintained that the function of God in all religions is to "act as a legitimating paradigm for the institution of patriarchy".

> IF MEN'S CLAIM TO PERSONHOOD IS BASED ON THE ASSUMPTION THAT THEY HAVE BEEN CREATED IN THE IMAGE OF GOD, THEN THROUGH THE PROCESS OF **POWER-OVER** THEY MARGINALIZE WOMEN AS NON-PERSONS, **IM**PERSONAL OBJECTS, "OTHER".

> I ADVISE FEMINISTS TO ADVOCATE THE NOTION OF GOD AS **IMMANENCE** AND TO DETACH GOD FROM GENDER.

MARY DALY

In her most famous book, *Gyn/Ecology* (1978), she rejected the term "God" altogether. She urged women to access the "wild woman" within them who will liberate them from social restrictions of feminine behaviour. Daly advocated revising language, which mainly represents men's experience of the world. She published a feminist dictionary, *Webster's First New Intergalactic Wickedary of the English Language* (1987).

# The 1980s

During the 1980s, feminist activity became the target of numerous attacks by academics, journalists and public speakers who told women that their struggle for equal rights had been won and was over.

Women were invited to return to their homes and perform their roles of mothers and wives while benefiting from the limited political and social rights they had earned.

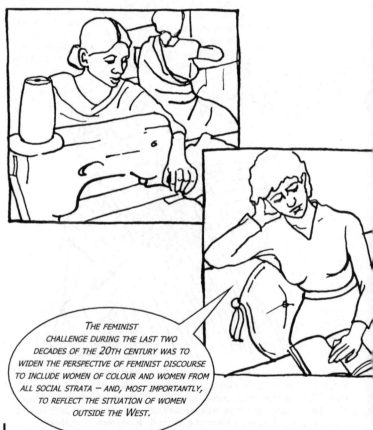

THE FEMINIST CHALLENGE DURING THE LAST TWO DECADES OF THE 20TH CENTURY WAS TO WIDEN THE PERSPECTIVE OF FEMINIST DISCOURSE TO INCLUDE WOMEN OF COLOUR AND WOMEN FROM ALL SOCIAL STRATA — AND, MOST IMPORTANTLY, TO REFLECT THE SITUATION OF WOMEN OUTSIDE THE WEST.

# Black Women's Experience of Feminism

Although first wave feminism professed to address all women's needs and concerns, yet it is not until the second wave that we begin to see public expressions of the significance of feminism to women of colour. In spite of a number of earlier female activists who spoke in public about the abolition of slavery in the US, it was only in the late 20th century that black women attempted to theorize the meaning of black feminism.

The central concern of black feminist thought is the inseparability of **race** and **gender**. Most black feminists refuse to see themselves as *women* first and foremost.

ABOVE LEFT: **ANGELA DAVIS** (B. 1944) IS AN AFRICAN AMERICAN FEMINIST ACTIVIST WHO IN THE 1970S WAS ASSOCIATED WITH THE POLITICAL ACTIVITIES OF THE BLACK PANTHERS. THIS ORGANIZATION WAS FOUNDED TO PROMOTE CIVIL RIGHTS AND SELF-DEFENCE.

ABOVE RIGHT: **ROSA PARKS** (1913–2005) WAS AN AFRICAN AMERICAN SEAMSTRESS WHO IN 1955 REFUSED TO GIVE UP HER SEAT ON THE BUS TO A WHITE PASSENGER. SHE WAS ARRESTED AND FINED. IT IS BELIEVED THAT HER ACT OF DEFIANCE INITIATED THE MODERN CIVIL RIGHTS MOVEMENT IN THE USA.

*WE, LIKE OTHER NON-WHITE WOMEN, READ OURSELVES IN TERMS OF OUR RACE, CLASS, EDUCATIONAL BACKGROUND AND SEXUAL ORIENTATION.*

Consequently, black feminism sets itself apart from mainstream feminist activity, which is seen as serving mainly middle-class, educated white women.

These ideas are illustrated in **Audre Lorde**'s explanation that, as a "forty-nine-year-old Black lesbian feminist socialist, mother of two, including one boy, and a member of an interracial couple", she did not want to divorce herself from any aspect of her identity in her feminist activism. Rather, Lorde concludes that in order to achieve a sense of Oneness, and escape the incessant feeling of Otherness ...

*... I WILL INTEGRATE ALL THE PARTS OF WHO I AM, OPENLY, ALLOWING POWER FROM PARTICULAR SOURCES OF MY LIVING TO FLOW BACK AND FORTH FREELY THROUGH ALL MY DIFFERENT SELVES, WITHOUT RESTRICTIONS OF EXTERNALLY IMPOSED DEFINITION.*

# Early Expressions of Black Feminism

**Sojourner Truth** (1797?–1883) was an American abolitionist who also advocated black women's rights. She began her speaking career as a preacher who toured the US helping freed slaves find work. In the 1850s, she became involved in the women's rights movement and added the fight for suffrage to that of freeing black slaves. Although she was illiterate, Truth dictated her autobiography to a friend and became a well known public figure who attracted large crowds.

# A'n't I a Woman?

Truth's most famous speech, "A'n't I a Woman?", was delivered at a convention on women's rights in 1851. In it, she is reported to have challenged a Protestant minister's claims that men deserve more privileges than women because they are intellectually superior and because God created Jesus as a man.

Her speech is often cited as an example of early black feminist political activism, although in many ways it is more about the status of the racialized and feminized body.

**Harriet Tubman** (1820?–1913) was probably the most militant black female activist of her time.

As an advocate of black women's rights, Tubman participated in the 1895 National Conference of Colored Women in America (NCCWA). She later became a strong supporter of women's suffrage. Tubman's life was rife with stories of disobedience and rebellion. However, she too was mostly interested in eradicating racial oppression and addressed issues of gender only when discussing the plight of black women. In recognition of her efforts, the US postal service issued a stamp to honour her as part of the Black Heritage series.

# Frances Harper

Many black female activists in the 19th century began their political life as abolitionists and added feminist activity to their agenda after the end of the American Civil War. Few of them seemed to differentiate between white women's feminism and their own. However, the case of **Frances E.W. Harper** (1825–1911) provides an example of the clash between race and gender which would come to characterize second wave black feminist activity.

Unlike Truth and Tubman, who were illiterate and born into slavery, Frances Harper was a highly educated lecturer, activist, poet and novelist.

*I WAS BORN INTO A FREED BLACK FAMILY AND EDUCATED AT THE PRESTIGIOUS ACADEMY FOR NEGRO YOUTH, WHERE I LEARNED GREEK, LATIN AND THE BIBLE.*

She achieved great fame as an intelligent and persuasive speaker, and was nicknamed the "Bronze Muse". She played an active part in the American Woman Suffrage Association and the National Council of Women. Wherever she lectured, Harper insisted on pleading the case of African American women in particular.

However, her relationship with white women activists was tested with the passing of the 15th Amendment of the US Constitution, which granted black men the vote. Stanton and Anthony were highly critical of this Amendment, and felt that white women were entitled to suffrage before black men. In this instance Harper's loyalty was to her race over her gender, and she broke the relationship with the white activists.

# The Combahee River Collective

Frances Harper's insistence on defining herself as a black American first and as woman next was written into one of the earliest manifestos of black feminism. The **Combahee River Collective** of black feminists initially met in 1974 with the aim of "defining and clarifying their politics".

WE ISSUED A STATEMENT IN 1982 ANNOUNCING OUR ACTIVE COMMITMENT TO STRUGGLE AGAINST RACIAL, SEXUAL, HETEROSEXUAL, AND CLASS OPPRESSION.

The statement underscored the participation of women of colour in second wave politics, and declared that only black women can identify their needs and write about their identities. It also declared that a collective and non-hierarchical distribution of power could pave the way for a revolutionary society in which oppression based on gender and sexual discrimination could be challenged and eradicated.

145

# Gynocentricism and Black Feminism

The Combahee collective coincided with the 1970s flourishing of **gynocentric** feminism, which recognized gender as an organizing principle of individual identity and social structures. Black feminist critics debated whether it was possible to articulate the distinctive experiences of black women by interacting with the experiences of other groups. Many critics, however, warned against adopting a separatist or exclusionary understanding of black feminism.

I'VE ALWAYS KNOWN THAT IF YOU WRITE FROM A BLACK EXPERIENCE, YOU'RE WRITING FROM A UNIVERSAL EXPERIENCE AS WELL ... I KNOW THAT YOU DON'T HAVE TO WHITEWASH YOURSELF TO BE UNIVERSAL.

SONIA SANCHEZ

# bell hooks

**bell hooks** (b. 1952) is one of the most prolific black feminist writers and social critics. The title of her first book, *Ain't I a Woman* (1981), was inspired by and clearly recalls Sojourner Truth's speech. It examined the marginalization of black women in contemporary feminist activism and theory. hooks associates her activism for achieving equal rights for women with her efforts to combat oppression.

*CONSEQUENTLY, I HAVE OFTEN ATTACKED MAINSTREAM WHITE FEMINISTS SUCH AS BETTY FRIEDAN AND NAOMI WOLF WHO DO NOT ENGAGE WITH ISSUES OF RACE AND CLASS IN THEIR WRITING.*

In her essays and speeches, hooks highlights the need to recognize and celebrate women's diversity and to fight against the "exclusionary use of the term feminism" by white middle-class women. She has famously urged women to stop declaring themselves to *be* feminists and to announce instead that they *advocate* feminism.

BELL HOOKS

# Alice Walker

**Alice Walker** (b. 1944) is perhaps the most widely read black American writer. She was heavily involved in the civil rights movement and published essays on the oppression of black American women.

> *I COINED THE TERM "**WOMANIST**", WHICH DENOTES A VERSION OF FEMINIST ACTIVITY SPECIFICALLY ADDRESSING THE CHALLENGES FACING BLACK WOMEN.*

ALICE WALKER

Walker published several works of fiction which caused controversy among black critics for their depiction of black men as sexist, violent husbands. She has often been accused of complicity with white stereotypes of black men, but has defended herself by claiming that her fiction attempts to highlight problems which have been long considered taboo.

Walker's publication of a collection of essays, *In Search of Our Mother's Gardens: Womanist Prose* (1983), ushered in an era of black gynocriticism, and she has influenced many feminist thinkers across the world.

MANY WOMEN IN DEVELOPING COUNTRIES WHO DO NOT ASCRIBE TO THE TENETS OF WHITE WESTERN FEMINISM HAVE FOUND THE TERM "WOMANIST" A USEFUL ALTERNATIVE TO DESCRIBING THEIR EFFORTS AT ACHIEVING EMANCIPATION AND FIGHTING FOR EQUALITY.

Walker defined a "womanist" as a "woman of color who was committed to the wholeness of the entire people, male and female". So the term becomes an alternative to "feminist" and expresses a collective notion of solidarity with one's culture and race as well as one's gender.

# Popular Fiction in the 1980s

In *The Female Eunuch*, Germaine Greer famously proclaimed that romance novels were the "opiate of the supermenial" and described the romantic hero as the "invention of women cherishing the chains of their own bondage". Romance stories published in women's magazines and in Mills and Boon novels generated a great deal of debate in the 1980s.

**Ann Douglas** dubbed the phenomenal increase in mass-market romance a symptom of "soft-porn culture".

*SHE THINKS THE INCREASE IN THE POPULARITY AND AVAILABILITY OF THESE NOVELS CAN BE CORRELATED WITH CONCERTED EFFORTS TO UNDERMINE THE RISE OF THE WOMEN'S MOVEMENT.*

However, other feminist critics questioned women's passivity as readers and refused to believe the suggestion that women believed and adopted the stereotypes offered to them in romance novels. **Tania Modleski** (b. 1949) is a Marxist feminist who writes about the representation of women in the popular media. Her first book, *Loving with a Vengeance* (1982), scrutinized traditional forms of writing which were aimed at women, such as Harlequin novels, Gothic romance and television soap operas.

# The Power of Romance

Modleski argued that reading romantic fiction can be a female expression of resistance. Romance novels typically tell the story of how a heartless and seemingly unfeeling man ends up falling in love and proposing to the heroine who has tamed and subdued him because of her virtue and purity.

*SUCH A PLOT ALLOWS MARRIED WOMEN, WHO ARE TRAPPED IN RELATIONSHIPS WHERE THEY FEEL UNLOVED AND UNCARED FOR, TO EXPERIENCE A SENSE OF EMPOWERMENT.*

TANIA MODLESKI

They can fantasize that their men, who take them for granted, are in fact mysterious romantic heroes who can be controlled only by their wives. This is a fantasy of power in which men are brought in line with women's desires.

# Feminism and Pornography

While the debate over the value of reading romance novels was relatively quiet and understated, feminists remain bitterly divided in their attitudes towards sexually explicit material in fiction and the media. They differ in their interpretation of the meaning and social function of pornography.

One group, the radical feminists, adopt an anti-pornography position which posits that all sexually explicit material is defamatory to women. **Andrea Dworkin** and **Catherine MacKinnon** are its key proponents. In the past, they have attempted to make the production of pornography a violation of civil rights.

ANDREA DWORKIN

*PORNOGRAPHY REVEALS THE IDEOLOGY OF MALE DOMINATION WHICH POSITS THAT MEN ARE SUPERIOR TO WOMEN BY VIRTUE OF THEIR PENISES ... THAT THE USE OF THE FEMALE BODY FOR SEXUAL OR REPRODUCTIVE PURPOSES IS A NATURAL RIGHT OF MEN.*

Anti-pornography campaigners argue that the availability of pornography in the written and visual media is linked to the sexual abuse of women in society.

Another group of feminists adopts a more libertarian position. In Britain, for example, the Black Lace imprint launched in 1993 was seen as a positive example of how pornographic material can be produced specially for a female audience. **Nancy Friday** is one critic who has made a career out of compiling and examining women's sexual fantasies. She aimed to deconstruct the angel/whore dichotomy by celebrating women's erotic pleasure in its various representations.

# Feminism and the Body

Second wave feminists challenged society's definition of femininity and its insistence on equating men with "mind" and women with nature and "body". As far back as the 1970s, feminists were aware of the power of the **male gaze** to objectify the female body by fixing it in photographs, paintings or other forms of artwork.

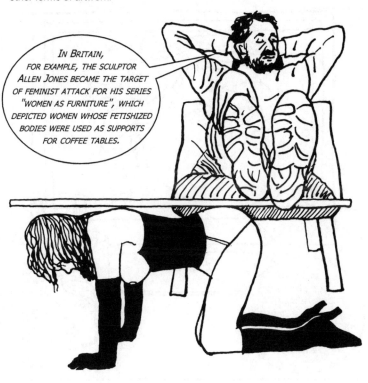

IN BRITAIN, FOR EXAMPLE, THE SCULPTOR ALLEN JONES BECAME THE TARGET OF FEMINIST ATTACK FOR HIS SERIES "WOMEN AS FURNITURE", WHICH DEPICTED WOMEN WHOSE FETISHIZED BODIES WERE USED AS SUPPORTS FOR COFFEE TABLES.

Feminist activists challenge these representations of traditional stereotypes of femininity because it is through the media that female consumers internalize gender identity.

In 1978, **Susie Orbach** published *Fat is a Feminist Issue*, in which she discussed eating disorders such as bulimia and anorexia as mechanisms for refusing sexual objectification. Orbach was the therapist of Lady Diana Spencer.

*I STRUGGLED TO GAIN OWNERSHIP OVER MY BODY, WHICH WAS CONTINUALLY PHOTOGRAPHED, DISCUSSED AND OBJECTIFIED BY THE MEDIA.*

In the 1980s, feminist activity revolved around attempts at **reclaiming** the female body by deconstructing the stereotypes and visual objects which defined it. Feminist critics became determined to identify and analyse the underlying **ideology** and the **social conditions** which produced images of women as commodities.

However, it was not until the 1990s that the debate over the representation of the female body was developed further and several theories about how women are "seen" by men were presented.

The British supermodel Kate Moss, who achieved fame because of her emaciated figure and youthful, innocent look, caused controversy in the ranks of feminist thinkers.

But whether it is the thin and slender or the shapely and voluptuous, the ideal female body has always been an object of fascination and fetishism.

# The Beauty Myth

In 1990, **Naomi Wolf** published the bestseller *The Beauty Myth: How Images of Beauty are Used Against Women*. She highlighted the strong influence of the media on women's perception of their bodies.

WOMEN EXPERIENCE FEELINGS OF INADEQUACY, SELF-HATRED AND IMPERFECTION ON BEING BOMBARDED WITH VISUAL REPRESENTATIONS OF THE "IDEAL BODY".

WHILE WOMEN HAVE ACHIEVED A GREAT DEAL OF PUBLIC INFLUENCE, THEY HAVE LOST THEIR PRIVATE RELATIONSHIP WITH THEIR BODY.

NAOMI WOLF

The fashion industry was the main culprit responsible for the rise in eating disorders and cosmetic surgeries. Wolf dubbed this phenomenon "the beauty myth", a form of backlash against the achievements of the feminist movement of the 1980s.

Although Wolf did not resolve the problem of the beauty myth in her first book, she later published *Fire with Fire* (1993), in which she clearly located the solution with women themselves. Wolf chastised women who indulge in what she called "**victim feminism**".

Her claim was controversial, especially to feminists who do not believe that women should fight "fire with fire", i.e. use men's tactics to fight men.

# The Grotesque

Feminism's understanding and theorizing of the female body remains a thorny issue, and one which is further complicated with theories about cross-dressing and postmodern conceptions of the **grotesque** body.

**Mikhail Bakhtin** defines the grotesque as any entity which transgresses the social order and is exiled into the margins of propriety and decorum.

MIKHAIL BAKHTIN

> *GROTESQUE BODIES ARE BODIES THAT EXIST OUTSIDE THE SOCIALLY ACCEPTED NORMS.*

**Mary Russo** argues that any practice which is seen as grotesque can be read as a "feminized" practice because the female body has traditionally been seen as corrupt and impure. The female body, which has been associated with blood, amniotic fluids and milk secretion, is often identified as the ultimate example of the grotesque.

Many artists and creative writers have used the grotesque body to illustrate its revolutionary potential, notably the English short story writer **Angela Carter**, who often appropriates images of the grotesque in her depiction of female bodies which do not conform to social expectations.

> I DEPLOY A WIDE RANGE OF GROTESQUE IMAGERY IN ORDER TO EXPOSE AND CRITIQUE THE PROCESSES INVOLVED IN CREATING ACCEPTABLE IMAGES OF THE "FEMININE" BODY.

ANGELA CARTER

THIS AND PREVIOUS PAGE FROM ANGELA CARTER'S *THE BLOODY CHAMBER*

# Feminism and the Question of Gender

Recently, a new discipline has emerged in academic circles under the heading "gender studies". The term implies a type of thinking about the dynamics of female and male experiences. In 1989 Elaine Showalter, who had previously campaigned for the practice of gynocriticism in order to unearth women's matrilineal literary tradition, declared that it was time to begin reading texts written by men.

*She says that women should read these texts not as illustrations of sexism and misogyny but as renditions of sexual difference.*

*And that they should study masculinity in the same way as they do femininity, seeing both as socially constructed roles.*

Showalter's approach to gender falls in line with other Anglo-American feminists, such as Ann Oakley, who distinguishes between sex (biology) and gender (social construction of feminine and masculine roles).

# Deconstructive Feminism

However, other feminist critics find this distinction problematic, notably **Judith Butler** (b. 1956), one of the most important contemporary theorists of deconstructive feminism. Her approach questions notions of "femaleness" which are taken for granted in society.

BUTLER ARGUES THAT GENDER DISTINCTIONS ARE VALID ONLY IF WE ACCEPT A SOCIAL SYSTEM BASED ON BINARY OPPOSITIONS: I.E., SEEING WOMAN AS **OPPOSED TO** MAN; "FEMININE" AS THE OPPOSITE OF "MASCULINE".

Butler disagrees with the sex/gender split by emphasizing the phenomenon of **cross-dressing** as an activity which challenges the neat distinction of sex and gender which heterosexual discourse has initiated. Cross-dressing provides the individual with a wider concept of gender identity which does not "normalize male/female dualism".

# Men Back at Centre Stage?

For her part, Tania Modleski takes issue with Showalter's invitation to pursue gender studies rather than women's studies, warning of the dangers involved in bringing "men back to the centre stage". In her book *Feminism Without Women: Culture and Criticism in a Postfeminist Age* (1991) she warned that the discipline of gender studies could deprive women of a crucial element of collective solidarity.

*THEY ARE BEING SCARED AWAY FROM THINKING OF THEIR IDENTITY AS WOMEN INTO THINKING ABOUT THEIR IDENTITY IN RELATION TO MEN.*

TANIA MODLESKI

Modleski reads the interest in gender studies as part of a **postfeminist** backlash against feminism.

# Girl Power

In the 1990s, the pop group the Spice Girls introduced the phenomenon of **girl power**, which asserted that women are sexual subjects who should lay claim to male privileges while performing their femininity. Girl power contradicted second wave feminism's assertion that fashion trends and traditional standards of physical beauty oppress and objectify women.

*Girl Power!!*

*WITH GIRL POWER, WE CAN USE SOCIETY'S EXPECTATIONS OF FEMALE BEHAVIOUR TO MANIPULATE PATRIARCHY AND ACHIEVE SUCCESS THROUGH FEMALE BONDING.*

Many feminists reacted vehemently to the rise of girl power, notably Germaine Greer, who attacked it in her book *The Whole Woman* (1999) on account of its cynical marketing of traditional trappings of sexualized femininity to young girls.

# Feminism and the Developing World

Oppressed women exist in many countries around the world. However, the discourse of Western feminism often relegates them to a marginal position, using universal labels such as "women in the Third World" to denote a rich variety of cultural, racial and class categories.

THE CATEGORIZATION OF THE HISTORY OF FEMINISM INTO "WAVES" WHICH ARE DELINEATED BY AMERICAN AND EUROPEAN EVENTS AND PERSONALITIES DOES NOT APPLY, NOR DOES IT REFLECT OUR CONDITION.

Feminist activists in developing countries resist social injustice against them in ways that often do not coincide with the feminist efforts that the West has witnessed. This sometimes leads to misunderstanding and misinterpretation of their struggle, their aims and goals.

Feminist theorists such as **Chandra Talpade Mohanty** attack the ways in which so-called "First World" feminists represent women in the "Third World". She notes that Western women are often depicted as strong, assertive individuals who are decisive and in control of their fate and of their bodies.

CHANDRA TALPADE MOHANTY

*WHEREAS WOMEN IN DEVELOPING COUNTRIES ARE INVARIABLY PORTRAYED AS VICTIMS OF A PATRIARCHAL ORDER WHICH ROBS THEM OF THEIR VOICE, DICTATES THEIR FATE, AND FORCES THEM INTO FINANCIAL DEPENDENCE.*

Mohanty condemns the West's misrepresentation of these women as sexually constrained, ignorant and helpless.

# The Subaltern

Another critical debate is raised by **Gayatri Spivak** in her conception of the "subaltern". Spivak denounces Western feminism for speaking **for** non-Western women and robbing them of a political voice. Such a practice marginalizes non-Western women and ignores their own efforts at countering social and political injustice.

GAYATRI SPIVAK

WHEN NON-WESTERN WOMEN SPEAK OR WRITE FROM WITHIN WESTERN CULTURE THEY SHATTER THE MYTH OF UNITY WHICH WESTERN FEMINISTS HAVE LONG CELEBRATED.

However, Spivak advises that such a different voice should not be seen as a threat to Western feminism; rather, this discourse of otherness should be incorporated and allowed to enrich the "imagined community of women" which Mohanty has identified.

# Challenging Rituals

Another branch of feminism in the developing world attempts to come to terms with specific social practices such as female circumcision, *saty* and "bride-pricing".

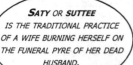

**SATY** OR **SUTTEE** IS THE TRADITIONAL PRACTICE OF A WIFE BURNING HERSELF ON THE FUNERAL PYRE OF HER DEAD HUSBAND.

IT WAS OUTLAWED BY THE BRITISH IN 1829 BUT CONTINUED IN REMOTE VILLAGES OF INDIA UNTIL RECENTLY.

*THE BRIDE-PRICE IS A SUM OF MONEY WHICH IS PAID BY THE GROOM IN EXCHANGE FOR HIS WIFE, AND IN RETURN FOR THE DOWRY SHE BRINGS WITH HER.*

Feminist activists such as **Nawal Saadawi** and **Fatima Mernissi** have written extensively on the complicated social and cultural implications of challenging rituals which are often mistakenly associated with religious practice. They have faced heavy criticism and sparked heated debates with their claims that female agency is often compromised for the sake of custom.

# What is Feminism?

*The Athenaeum*, 27 April 1895, defined a feminist as a woman who "has in her the capacity of fighting her way back to independence".

"Men and Women who are politically engaged in feminist issues should avoid labelling themselves as feminists; rather they should substitute 'I am a feminist' with 'I advocate feminism' to emphasize the ideological basis of their beliefs." (bell hooks)

"I AM NOT A BARBIE DOLL" (worded sign hoisted by a young girl in the 1970 Women's Strike for Equality march)

"Feminism asks the world to recognize at long last that women aren't decorative ornaments, worthy vessels, members of a 'special-interest' group." (Susan Faludi)

*FEMINISM'S AGENDA IS BASIC: IT ASKS THAT WOMEN NOT BE FORCED TO CHOOSE BETWEEN PUBLIC JUSTICE AND PRIVATE HAPPINESS.*

SUSAN FALUDI

"Womanist is to feminist as purple to lavender." (Alice Walker)

"I am a feminist, and what that means to me is much the same as the meaning of the fact that I am Black: it means that I must undertake to love myself and to respect myself as though my very life depends upon self-love and self-respect." (June Jordan)

"Let woman then go on – not asking favors, but claiming as a right the removal of all hindrances to her elevation in the scale of being – let her receive encouragement for the proper cultivation of all her powers, so that she may enter profitably into the active business of life." (Lucretia Mott)

# Milestones

**1645** Britain hangs witches
**1646** Massachusetts and Connecticut colonies execute witches
**1650** English and US Puritan laws on adultery
**1700** In Berlin, unmarried women are forced to pay a special tax
**1792** Mary Wollstonecraft publishes *A Vindication of the Rights of Woman*
**1832** Britain passes Reform Bill extending voting rights to the middle class
**1837** Mary Lyon founds Mount Holyoke Female Seminary to educate women in New England
**1839** Mississippi passes first US married women's property law in America
Infant Custody Act passed in Britain
**1847** In Britain, labour law restricts women and children to working a maximum of ten hours a day
**1848** Seneca Falls Convention
Queen's College for women opens in London
**1857** Divorce and Matrimonial Causes Act establishes civil divorce court in London
**1858** Elizabeth Blackwell becomes first accredited female physician in Britain and the US
**1869** National Woman Suffrage Association Created
Girton College for Women opens in Cambridge
**1870** Married Women's Property Act passed in Britain
British Education Act of 1870 allows women to attend university but not obtain degrees
**1871** Victoria Woodhull runs for President of the US
**1876** British medical schools opened to women
**1879** Women's College opens at Oxford Radcliffe
**1892** Women vote in New Zealand
**1895** The word "feminist" is first used in a book review in *The Athenaeum*
**1903** Women's Social and Political Union is formed
**1906** London *Daily Mail* coins the term "suffragette"
The National Federation of Women Workers is founded in the UK
**1907** Women can be elected onto borough and county councils under the Qualification of Women Act (UK)
**1908** A gathering in support of women's suffrage in Hyde Park, London attracts 250,000 people
**1909** First woman suffrage parade held in New York
White Slave Traffic Act passed to outlaw the transatlantic transport of women for "immoral purposes"
**1915** The first Women's Institute in Britain is founded in North Wales
**1916** First birth control clinic opens in the US
**1918** Women over 30 are granted the right to vote in Britain

| 1922 | The Law of Property Act allows both husband and wife to inherit property equally in Britain |
|---|---|
| 1928 | All women in Britain gain equal voting rights with men |
| 1939 | Term "Rosie the Riveter" is coined, referring to women employed in American defence industries |
| 1950 | United Nations drafts conventions on women's rights |
| 1956 | The Sexual Offences Act in Britain defines rape under specific criteria |
| 1960 | The first oral contraceptive is developed in the USA |
| 1961 | US commission on the status of women is created |
| | The Pill is approved by the US Food and Drug Administration |
| 1966 | National Organization for Women Founded in the US |
| 1967 | The contraceptive pill becomes available in Britain |
| 1968 | Miss America protest |
| | In Britain, female workers at the Ford Plant in Dagenham strike over equal pay, leading to the passing of the Equal Pay Act |
| 1969 | First Women's Studies programme started at San Diego University |
| 1970 | The First National Women's Liberation Conference in held in Britain at Ruskin College. The Women's Liberation Movement begins |
| | Miss World Competition is interrupted by feminist protestors |
| 1971 | *Ms* magazine is founded |
| 1972 | *Spare Rib* is founded |
| 1975 | The Sex Discrimination Act guarantees equal treatment of men and women at work, in education and training (Britain) |
| | The Employment Protection Act introduces maternity leave (Britain) |
| | The National Abortion Campaign is formed in Britain |
| 1977 | The First Rape Crisis Centre opens in London |
| 1978 | The Women's Aid Federation of Northern Ireland is established |
| | The Organisation of Women of African and Asian Descent is set up |
| 1979 | The journal *Feminist Review* is founded |
| 1984 | The national Black Feminist Conference is held in Britain |
| 1985 | The first black lesbian conference is held in Britain |
| | Prohibition of Female Circumcision Act |
| 1987 | The Feminist Majority Foundation is created and campaigns for women's education, protection and health |
| 1994 | Violence Against Women Act passed |
| 1996 | Northern Ireland's Women's Coalition is founded |
| 2000 | The US Supreme Court invalidates portions of the Violence Act Against Women, permitting victims of rape, domestic violence, etc. to sue their attackers in a federal court |
| 2001 | The London Partnerships Register, allowing lesbian and gay individuals and unmarried heterosexual couples to register their partnerships |
| 2002 | In Britain, Parliament passes measures allowing lesbian and unmarried couples to adopt children |
| 2005 | The first civil registration of same-sex couples takes place |

# Further Reading

Rosemary Tong, *Feminist Thought: A More Comprehensive Introduction* (2nd edn), published by Westview Press (1998) is an indispensable text which provides critiques of the main schools of feminist thought.

Sarah Gamble's re-edited *The Routledge Companion to Feminism and Postfeminism* (2001) contains critical essays and a glossary of key terms.

Linda Nicholson's *The Second Wave: A Reader in Feminist Theory* (1997) includes key primary readings from feminist critics, prefaced by lucid critical analyses of their ideas.

*The Feminist Papers From Adams to de Beauvoir*, edited by Alice S. Rossi (1988), is an invaluable collection of essays and speeches from leading feminist thinkers.

An indispensable textbook is Mariam Fraser and Monica Greco's *The Body* (2005), which is a compilation of key essays on the representation of the body in literature, the popular media and in various cultures.

## Additional references

Betterton, Rosemary, *An Intimate Distance: Women, Artists and the Body* (London: Routledge, 1996)

Brooks, Ann, *Postfeminisms: Feminism, Cultural Theory and Cultural Forms* (London: Routledge, 1990)

Bulbeck, Chilla, *Re-Orienting Western Feminisms: Women's Diversity in a Postcolonial World* (Cambridge University Press, 1998)

Chedzgoy, Kate, et. al. (eds), *Voicing Women: Gender and Sexuality in Early Modern Writing* [1996] (Edinburgh University Press, 1998)

Davies, Miranda, *Third World – Second Sex* (London: Sen Books, 1983)

Dworkin, Andrea, *Pornography: Men Possessing Women* (New York: Perigee, 1981)

El Saadawi, Nawal, *The Hidden Face of Eve: Women in the Arab World* [1972] (London: Zed Books, 1980)

Jaggar, Alison, et. al. (eds), *A Companion to Feminist Philosophy* (Oxford: Blackwell, 1998)

Marks, Elaine and Isabelle de Courtivron (eds), *New French Feminisms* (Brighton: Harvester, 1981)

Mernissi, Fatima, *Women and Islam* [1987] (Oxford: Blackwell, 1991)

Mitchell, Susan, *The Matriarchs: Twelve Australian Women Talk About Their Lives* (Melbourne: Penguin, 1987)

Russo, Mary, *The Female Grotesque: Risk, Excess and Modernity* (London: Routledge, 1995)

Spivak, Gayatri Chakravorty, *In Other Words: Essays in Culture and Politics* (New York: Methuen, 1987)

Wajcman, Judy, *Feminism Confronts Technology* (Cambridge: Polity, 1991)

Wieringa, Saskia (ed.), *Subversive Women – Women's Movements in Africa, Asia, Latin America and the Caribbean* (Delhi: Kali for Women, 1995)

# About the author and artist

**Cathia Jenainati** is Associate Professor in English and Comparative Literary Studies at the University of Warwick (England). She teaches courses on American and Canadian literature and feminist literary theory.

**Judy Groves** is a painter and illustrator. She has illustrated many of the Icon *Introducing* series, including *Wittgenstein*, *Lacan*, *Plato*, *Chomsky*, *Philosophy* and *Political Philosophy*.

# Acknowledgements

### Author's Acknowledgements
I wish to thank Helen Sampson (formerly of Icon Books) for this commission, as well as Duncan Heath for his patience and meticulous editing of the text. My thanks also to members of my two families, the Jenainatis and van Nieuwerburghs, for their continuing support and unconditional love.

### Artist's Acknowledgements
Many thanks to Oscar Zarate for the illustration on page 85. Thanks also to Minnie Stolboff, Linda Knutson and Kaiya Waerea for allowing me to use them as models for some of the poses.

# Index